Organisational Communication: The Role of the HR Professional

Paul Turner is group HR business director for Lloyds TSB and a vice president of the Chartered Institute of Personnel and Development. He has experience of working in both human resources and general management in the banking, telecommunications and health sectors in the UK. His international assignments include a period living and working in Hong Kong, taking responsibility for markets in China and Japan, as well as business development covering Europe, Africa and India. He also worked in marketing financial trading systems in New York, Frankfurt and London. Paul obtained a first degree from the University of East Anglia and a PhD from the University of Sheffield. He is a visiting professor at Nottingham Business School and a fellow of the CIPD. He has published many articles and has spoken at conferences in Paris, Geneva, Montreux and Nashville, as well as the CIPD national conferences in Harrogate. Paul Turner is the author of *HR Forecasting and Planning*, also published by the CIPD. Paul is 50, married with two children and lives in Chesterfield, Derbyshire.

The Chartered Institute of Personnel and Development is the leading publisher of books and reports for personnel and training professionals, students, and for all those concerned with the effective management and development of people at work. For details of all our titles, please contact the Publishing Department:

tel. 020–8263 3387
fax 020–8263 3850
e-mail publish@cipd.co.uk
The catalogue of all CIPD titles can be viewed on the CIPD website:
www.cipd.co.uk/bookstore

Organisational Communication: The Role of the HR Professional

Paul Turner

Chartered Institute of Personnel and Development

Design by Beacon GDT
Typesetting by Fakenham Photosetting Ltd, Fakenham, Norfolk
Printed in Great Britain by The Cromwell Press, Trowbridge, Wiltshire

British Library Cataloguing in Publication Data
A catalogue record for this book is available from the British Library

ISBN 0–85292–962 5

To Robert Foss, Elisabeth Barber, Georgie Hodgson, Eila Rana, Steve Riley, Catryn Hemlock,
Barry Bloch, Steve Crabbe, Mike Watts, Gail Turner, Rita Sammons, Norman Mitchinson,
Bruce Thew, Pat Holroyd, Alf Worsfold, Georgina Mace.

This book is dedicated to the greatest communicator of the past 100 years: John Lennon

Learning Resources
Centre

1248081 9

Chartered Institute of Personnel and Development, CIPD House,
Camp Road, London SW19 4UX
Tel: 020–8971 9000   Fax: 020–8263 3333
E-mail: cipd@cipd.co.uk Website: www.cipd.co.uk
Incorporated by Royal Charter. Registered Charity No. 1079797

Contents

Introduction

In his novel *Breakfast of Champions* the great American author Kurt Vonnegut tells the story of an alien called Zog from the planet Margo. Zog has all sorts of valuable information, including cures for diseases and the solution for how to end war. Zog lands at night in Connecticut. Having touched down he sees a house on fire and rushes to tell the owners how to put out the fire. Yes, he even knows how to do this! But Zog can only communicate by farting and tap-dancing, which he does to the owner of the burning house. On seeing the farting, tap-dancing alien, the owner brains him with a golf club. Couldn't understand him, you see. There is a moral to this story: it's no use having the solution if we can't communicate it!

Such a moral is pretty obvious. So what's all the fuss about?

Well, it's because there are polarised views about the subject. On the one hand, communication is seen as flimflam and floss, spin and sound-bite. At best, it's form without substance, at worst, hypocrisy and economy with the truth. The political communicator is now seen as a spin doctor, mostly a pejorative description; the organisational communicator is struggling with a disengaged and cynical workforce. *But*, on the other hand, we see the communicator as a great leader: Jack, Tony, Richard and Maggie – strategist or 'e' success story – funky businessmen or women whose brilliance at communication creates an empowered, informed population.

These are two starkly contrasting pictures of communication. Two pictures that make you sit up and take notice. That sometimes bring a smile of satisfaction. That sometimes make you wince. But we do know that communication is one of the most fundamental actions that links one human being to another. It is the fibre that binds together social relationships. It is the basis of progress in our society. For those who work in organisations, effective communication is a necessary precursor to the delivery of strategy, change, employee commitment and, ultimately, competitive advantage. This is why former New York City Mayor Rudolph Giuliani said at the 2002 SHRM conference in Philadelphia that communication was one of his five main tenets of leadership (*People Management* 11 July 2002). We might agree with the comment that 'communication is the lifeblood of the organisation. It is a business requirement, not just a matter of good human relations' (Adair 1997).

It's also an increasing requirement of the HR professional. The ability of the organisation to engage a multitude of stakeholders through excellent communication strategy and action is now an essential competence. Without it, the chances of the organisation ever achieving its strategic objectives are reduced. Poor communication will not be tolerated by employees, managers, the board, the media or the City. Those in HR who have had a passing relationship with communication are now being asked to embrace it wholeheartedly. So it's incumbent on us at all levels of the HR function, and indeed all disciplines, to become conversant with the principles and practices of organisational communication. If we are to achieve the thing that Clive Morton talks about in his excellent book *Leading HR,* that is 'trust, social glue and networks', we shall need to deliver effective communication also (Morton, Newall and Sparkes 2001).

Let's start with the most critical part of the communication role of the HR professional: employee engagement. If we accept that uncertainty is a major demotivator, then communication about current and future performance should be seen as an absolute priority for the organisation. This is true even when conditions are stable. But when was the last time this happened? So 'the reality is that in times of uncertainty organisations need more than just compliance from employees. They need to engage people's hearts and minds, gain their energy and commitment and get them focusing their efforts in the right direction' (Quirke 2002). An effective communication programme is key to this.

Let's move on to other stakeholders. The board and the senior management team will demand of HR a well-thought-out and well-communicated strategy. The media will want to know about key events as they concern people, and the City will need convincing that the organisation's people strategies are as sound as their financial strategies. All of these point in the same direction: HR has to get its communications act together!

This book is intended to introduce some ideas about how communication can be integrated into the role of the HR professional, as well as some techniques for doing so. It is intended as a guide. It is not intended as the definitive guide. There is a good body of work on communication in its most general definition that will support the implementation of communication plans that are effective, value-adding and of strategic importance – objectives that are key to HR's involvement in the organisational communication process.

THE STRUCTURE OF THE BOOK

The book is divided into four parts. The first (Chapters 1–3) is about 'the organisation and change: the role of communication', and traces the background to organisational communication and HR's growing role in it. The second (Chapters 4–7) describes the principles and uses of communication in an organisational context. The third part (Chapters 8–10) deals with external communication and how HR should be involved – either directly or working with the organisation's PR experts. Part 4 covers aspects of internal communication and the various HR contributions to this area (Chapters 11–13). Chapter 14 will conclude the book by summarising the main points of learning.

In the first chapter I look at the growing importance of communication in the modern organisation and set the scene for HR's involvement in the field.

The second chapter of the book puts the whole issue of HR communication in context by looking at the changing role of HR. This is important because a clear definition of what HR does in the modern organisation is a prerequisite for delivering effective communication.

Chapter 3 discusses some of the external factors that are having an impact on the organisation, and how communication is delivered. In particular this chapter considers why the emphasis on communication has changed and how social, technological and organisational factors have raised the game for communication. Finally, the impact of these factors on organisational communication is discussed.

Chapter 4 introduces the principles of communication in their generality.

Chapter 5 acts as a resumé for organisational communication, outlining the theoretical basis for communication, the various models of communication that have been put forward and some research findings into the efficacy of particular types of communication.

Chapters 6 and 7 provide a framework for developing an HR communication strategy and the component parts of the communication plan. These two activities are prerequisites for the more detailed work that goes with each HR 'segment', whether this is an employee group, the media or the board.

The three external groups with whom the HR professional is likely to have an interface, and therefore a communication requirement, are potential employees, the media and the City. Two of these, the media and the City, are relatively faint on the radar of HR because they have been dealt with largely by other parts of the organisation (most notably the press office and the finance department). Potential employees have, of course, been a natural source of interface for HR through recruitment. However, the demands from this group have changed because of the war for talent. Now, we may ask the question, does the war for talent still hold true? I've worked on the assumption that it does, although it may be relevant to talk about the recruitment and retention of key employee groups, as recent CIPD research has suggested.

Chapter 8 focuses on the need to 'trade up' on how the company's employment proposition is presented to potential employees. The job advert in the local or national press is no longer a guarantee that the organisation will be able to recruit its quota of talent. In a world where talent is in short supply there is a need to develop new techniques for and approaches to the labour market, most notably the employment brand.

Chapter 9 focuses on the role of HR in the organisation's relationship with the City. It outlines how analysts and investors are focusing on people issues in several areas. Talent management and succession, employment levels, productivity and labour costs are increasingly the subject of analyst questioning. The HR professional needs to know, therefore, how to present these in a way that satisfies this particular group.

Chapter 10 deals with an equally challenging role, that of HR's relationship with the media. The 'company spokesperson' on industrial action, a juicy employment tribunal or a culturally stretching piece of European legislation may well have been someone from the public relations department or a senior general manager. However, there is a growing demand for those in HR to fulfil this role; how to communicate with the media is a competence that the HR professional has to develop.

Having dealt with communication in an external context, the book then focuses on internal communication.

Chapter 11 deals with the subject of employee communication. This goes well beyond the traditional staff notice. The need to communicate and, most importantly, engage employees is now critical. A new psychological contract has emerged over the past few years that has emanated from both the changing demands of the employer and that of the employee in equal measure. It is not enough just to let employees know what is going on. They have to understand, believe and buy into the organisation's direction and strategy. Nothing less than full engagement will deliver sustained organisational success. Of all the challenges facing the HR professional, this is likely to be the most difficult.

Before HR can deliver its strategy it has to gain sign-off from the board. In the past this was an act of faith. Now it isn't. The board will want to see a strategic view from HR that is aligned with the business strategy. It will want to see well-thought-out financial business cases for its investment in HR. It will want to see a return on its time and money. Chapter 12 investigates how HR might best communicate its arguments to the board and the issues involved in this concept of board-level human resources.

Finally, Chapter 13 addresses the issue of communication within HR itself. This is important for two reasons. First, because the increasingly specialist nature of HR functions (dealing with the equally specialised nature of the employment relationship, industrial relations, reward, and learning, training and development etc) lends itself to fragmented, unrelated offerings from HR. We have to make sure that this doesn't happen, and that HR is 'joined up' in its solutions to business issues. Second, it is important because the organisation itself is expecting a single, coherent proposition from the HR function. It is expecting its talent and succession strategy to be dealt with by related training and reward strategies, and its employee relations strategy to be supported by good communication.

In addressing the various facets of communication in this way, the book is intended to give the HR professional at least some tools and techniques to deal with the growing demands on his or her communication skills.

Part 1

The organisation and change: the role of communication

1

Vibration and frequencies – the importance of communication in the organisation

No matter what anybody tells you, words and ideas can change the world. Dead Poets Society (1989)

Given recent revelations of corporate impropriety, with the resultant fall-out in terms of economic uncertainty and failure, the issue of how we manage people within organisations has re-emerged with a vengeance. This issue is not simply one of minimising financial risk and enhancing control but more fundamentally a cultural issue of ethics, performance and commitment. While these may sound like 'faddish' concepts from the 1990s, their relevance to today has been reinforced by an economy where the old rules and expectations of business and investment no longer apply. In an environment where you can no longer look for the easy way out, the 'soft stuff' in organisations is increasingly being recognised as the hardest to deliver and central to a healthy balance-sheet.

So if the opportunity to put people at the heart of the organisation is increasingly apparent, why is it that the human resource and internal communications functions typically continue to be reactive and operational? Why do they often appear to invest a disproportionate amount of time and energy in face-saving, gate-keeping and political game-playing?

The future success for these two teams must be in the opportunity to provide one people-centred solution. In reality these two functions are part of delivering a single answer: to deliver the organisation's capability to effectively lead people through change. It is increasingly critical that human resources and internal communications work together to support their organisation and its leaders. Leadership is tough enough, and 'follower-ship' is no longer guaranteed. Having a two-way, ongoing, engaging and adult dialogue is essential. The people-centred specialists in organisations have the skills, experience and opportunities to facilitate this dialogue. By doing so they can help minimise the risks of improper behaviour by increasing transparency, while increasing people's sense of engagement and commitment to the organisation and its purpose. Ultimately this dialogue will also enhance a company's ability to drive up its revenues and drive down its costs. This proposal may seem simple; however, the implementation is not. Getting past old mental models and ways of working may actually be the easy part. Learning to work together on

a business agenda is the real challenge for the human resource and internal communications teams.
Barry Bloch, BA SocSc, BA (Hons), MA CPsychol Partner, Smythe Dorward Lambert Limited

INTRODUCTION

The principal purpose of this book is to provide commentary, tools and techniques to HR professionals on the subject of organisational communication. For many this will have been an area of interest that is somehow slightly distant from HR. But, as we shall see, this perspective is changing, and changing rapidly. The growing importance of communication in our lives means that it is no longer possible to separate communication from human relations: it is right in the ballpark of the HR professional. This is not just about the Web, revolutionary though this may have once been. It is about the daily diet of news from terrestrial and satellite broadcasting channels and company intranets. It is about the massive choice in traditional forms of communication through newspapers and journals. And it is about our expectations that we will be communicated with – whatever the subject, whatever the time and wherever we are. Where demand for news and individual expectations increases, and where sources of news supply increase also, the communication equilibrium reaches a higher level. This is what we are facing as providers of HR expertise in the organisation: an unprecedented demand for communication which, when translated into organisational terms, means that we have to respond in kind.

Communication is no longer the simple transmission of a message (if it ever was). It is a force for change. It is a powerful, impactful force that resonates throughout our working lives.

'COMMUNICATING WITH IMPACT'

There is power in communication. Take two contrasting examples. The first was a speech given in 1963 by President John F Kennedy in Berlin. He said, 'Today, in the world of freedom, the proudest boast is *ich bin ein Berliner*.' This was in response to the Soviet threat in an era of Cold War. It was what the people wanted to hear and they were 'swept by a surge of pride and warmth, and deeply stirred as few such massive audiences in history have ever been moved' (O'Donnell, Powers and McCarthy 1972). This was a famous speech in a desperate historical context: communication with a powerful impact delivered by a great orator, a dramatic example of human communication.

But communication can also be effective in less dramatic circumstances. In sharp contrast, the second example took place outside Marble Arch Underground Station in 2002. The *Evening Standard* advertising hoarding proclaimed 'ASTEROID ON COLLISION COURSE WITH EARTH'. It was, as things turned out, a vague possibility 17 years hence. But people still stopped to read the headline. The thing that linked these two events was that both were communication with impact. OK, they are separated by 40 years in which the world has changed dramatically, but both achieved the same objective. They communicated a message that grabbed the attention of an audience.

We can see that if a message, however great or small, is to be conveyed, a combination of things has to be in place. What we know about Kennedy's speech and other examples of great communication is that when the media, timing, the location, the individual and the language of communication come together, the result can be dramatic. We know from it that the way we communicate has to be audience-specific. And we know that the message has to have some

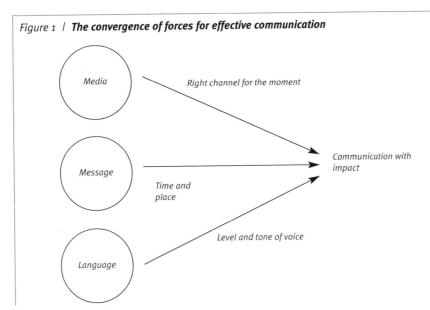

Figure 1 / **The convergence of forces for effective communication**

relevance, some meaning and some interest to those listening. So, even when communication is not as dramatic as a John F Kennedy speech, there are some consistent 'rules for success'. In the *Evening Standard* headline the point was about grabbing the attention of the audience as a means of engaging with them and (hopefully) leading them to purchase the product. Understanding these rules and knowing how to apply them is important. There are lessons that we have to learn if we are to deal with some of today's communication challenges. Figure 1 shows how all these things come together.

Where there is a convergence of media, message and language, it is possible to achieve communication with impact. So, those who are involved in communication in an organisational context have to take account of each element. Spending time gaining sign-off to a communication from the various stakeholders (each of whom will inevitably have a different view!) in the preparation of a brilliant message but not having the means to get the message to the intended audience is a total waste. Preparing a message, getting the delivery channels in place and yet neglecting 'tone of voice', ie the language in which the message is couched, likewise does not achieve its objectives. So we have to work on a holistic view of communication, making sure that each part is integrated with and complementary to the others.

But, you may ask, how are such lessons relevant to a book about HR? The answer is simple. They're relevant to HR because HR now have to pick up communication responsibilities that were previously in the domain of other departments.

GIVING A VOICE AS WELL AS EARS TO EMPLOYEES AND OTHER STAKEHOLDERS

Why has this occurred? Why is it such an issue? The pace of change in the contemporary organisation, the revolution in information availability created by (but not exclusively through) the Internet, and the increased importance of people to competitive advantage have all converged to heighten awareness of communication in the contemporary organisation. *Effective communication is now seen as a precursor to effective performance.* Chief executive officers are demanding that more attention be given to 'people' communication. This has, in turn, led to a growing involvement of HR professionals in the area. But this isn't communication in any traditional sense. Far from it. This is a more sophisticated form: a process that has 'engagement' as its objective and that uses a range of channels in its transmission. Nowadays communication is seen 'less as a craft industry and more of a profession' (Quirke 2002). So there is a growing demand for those in HR to develop new communication skills – once the sole province of PR staff, external communication agencies, corporate relations departments and marketing! There is plenty of evidence to convince us that the need to communicate effectively is no longer an incidental activity for those in HR. It is now a core competence. The reason for this is the pressing need to engage employees and other stakeholders in the strategy and beliefs of the organisation.

The return on investment in communication can be significant and lead to a contribution to success. Not doing so can be equally significant. Recently, lack of communication was identified as:

> *a big problem for companies trying to adapt in today's ever-evolving marketplace. A study by Stephan Erbschloe at the University of Denver found that poor communication and political infighting were the two top factors that slowed change in 46 companies setting up Internet businesses.* Grensing-Pophal 2002

But what does communication mean in this new environment? It is now recognised as a dynamic two-way flow rather than a unidirectional passing on of information. *This means giving a voice as well as ears to employees.* It means satisfying the media and the City about the efficacy of the organisation's people strategy and practice. And it means satisfying the board as to the wisdom of its investment in the organisation's human capital. Yet we still have divergent views about what we mean by communication and the value of dealing with communication issues in a strategic way.

WHY WE NEED TO COMMUNICATE

The necessity to get communication right should be considered a critical success factor for the organisation. It has become harder, though, because of changes in the world of work over the past few years. This means that employees are no longer locked-in lifers subject to command-and-control management. They are mobile, informed and less likely to put up with superficial communications claptrap. They will demand to know what's going on, where the organisation is heading and what role they have in it. The internal communicator now has to play a major part in providing this information, not as a photocopier of information but as an 'adviser with teeth' (Smythe 2002). For the employer the challenge is threefold:

- to make sure that everyone who is a stakeholder in the organisation understands the direction, the strategy, the operational context and the performance

- to make sure that everyone who is a stakeholder understands and accepts what is expected of them in this environment

- to protect and enhance the organisation's image.

In short, this is a matter of communicating with impact: 'expressing thoughts, feelings, and ideas effectively in individual and group situations; presenting ideas effectively; clearly expressing ideas … adjusting language to the characteristics and needs of the audience' (Byham, Smith and Paese 2000).

BUT WHY HR?

All very interesting, you may say. Is this itself some kind of spin about communication? And, even if we accept its importance, what's it got to do with HR? Why should people who work in HR be interested in communication if it's such a hassle? Surely we aren't being asked to take on Charlie Whelan's mantle? We aren't qualified to do such a thing – are we? It seems to be a no-win situation. Why not let someone else, far better qualified in, say, marketing or public relations, take responsibility for communication?

In spite of the apparent confusion about this new challenge, there are good reasons for HR professionals to take on more organisational communication. We know, as outlined in Figure 2, that there is a very strong link between HRM and performance. We also know that putting this into practice is very difficult: HR issues still have a long way to go before they get the right amount of air time with the management of the organisation. And we know that there is a huge challenge getting these messages through to the workforce. So HR communication is an immensely important area of HR strategy and practice. But this means that we in HR have to get our act together. First we have to clarify our role in the organisation. Then we have to understand the contribution of organisational communication to this role. Finally we have to develop some new skills to fulfil the challenge. But what is the context for this growing interest in communication?

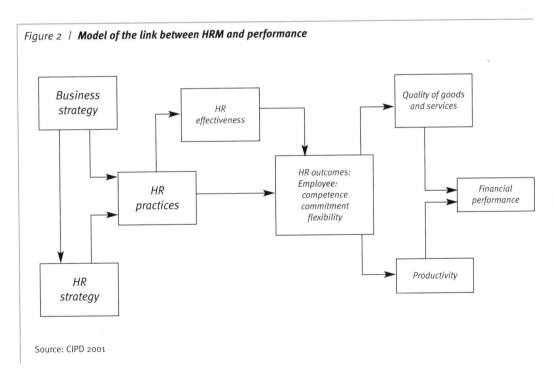

Figure 2 | *Model of the link between HRM and performance*

Source: CIPD 2001

VIBRATION AND FREQUENCIES

Communication is back in vogue. The reason? Because it's becoming harder and harder to get across a message in a world that is complex, ever-changing and riddled with discontinuity. For those who work in organisations, particularly Western ones, there has been a rather dramatic re-evaluation of the way we work (Sampson 1995). In this new way, communication is vital as both a strategic contributor to competitive advantage and as a genuine management issue.

Let's look at this issue and how it affects the world of work. Something profound has happened to change the nature of work and workers. It has also questioned the traditional ways in which we communicate. Such change has happened at the very time when the nature of communication is itself changing. On the one hand there has been an increase in both the quality and volume of information *outside* the organisation. This means that there is a heightened expectation for information *inside* the organisation – a demand that will not be satisfied by the staff notice-board. On the other hand the technological media to deliver such information are at an advanced level and available to more and more people.

Even at its most basic level – the giving out of messages by one person and the receiving and understanding of those messages by another – there is more complexity. The diverse, pluralist nature of modern society and the organisation means that there is no longer a communication style that is universal. We have to understand 'the vibration and the frequencies we create ... the harmonics of the organisation', as well as those overt obvious pieces of information (*Fast Company* June 2002). There's no doubt that this is a real challenge. Communication has become more difficult.

Furthermore, it's no longer a matter of just the communication process. It's also how we communicate. To quote a recent article in the *Sunday Times,* success depends on a new style of internal communication that is less about 'telling' and more about 'engaging'. 'If people understand the bigger organisational picture they will be more willing to stay for the ride and more motivated to do the job you need them to do' (*Sunday Times* 28 April 2002). It is an important and complex subject that demands attention from those in HR. On the one hand it is necessary for all managers to have effective communication competence if they are to be successful and deliver their objectives. Indeed, the 'manager who suffers from poor communication skills is likely to feel frustrated most of the time. And he is even more likely to be surrounded by a number of unhappy and unproductive subordinates' (Andrews and Baird 1989). On the other hand John Adair, writing about communication at the highest level, argues that:

> Communication is a dimension or a facet of almost all that a leader does. A leader communicates in order to achieve the common task, to build the team and to meet individual needs ... In the context of leadership, to communicate means to share with or impart to others one's thoughts and information in order to obtain a desired response ... the primary responsibility for good communication lies with the leader. Adair 1989

In leadership, communication is 'the art of inspiring while informing'. But, of particular interest to those in HR, there is the viewpoint that communication has gone beyond the area of the gifted amateur to that of the trained professional.

So communication can be a dramatic characteristic of successful leadership or an everyday part of organisational activity. To some, 'communication is everything ... most of our needs and indeed most of what makes us human has communication as its root' (Rouse and Rouse 2002).

GETTING ORGANISATIONAL COMMUNICATION RIGHT

In today's organisation,

> *most managers ... understand the strategic implications of the information-based, knowledge-driven, service-intensive economy. They know what the new game requires: speed, flexibility and continuous self-renewal. They even are recognising that skilled and motivated people are central to the operations of any company that wishes to flourish in the new age.* Bartlett and Ghoshal 2002

Communication is all part of the success path in this new economic reality.

It has to satisfy a broad range of organisational stakeholders and their information demands. When an organisation is unable to adjust to the requirements of the new knowledge environment it can have devastating effects. It's so tough to get this engagement process going that people are even talking about 'workplace marketing', which is 'a strategic marketing activity executed within the organisational fabric and with the objective of creating an exceptional customer experience' (Mumby-Croft and Williams 2002). This approach regards workplace marketing as a strategic management tool intended to 'address the challenges of implementation' of strategy and change. To do so will require an integrated approach to organisational communication. Figure 3 shows a process that demonstrates how this may be achieved. What this figure explains is the interrelationship between internal and external influences and the need to take a holistic view of these if effective 'workplace marketing' is to occur. The employee will only engage in the culture and standards of the organisation – and be a party to achieving competitive advantage – if there is engagement at several levels.

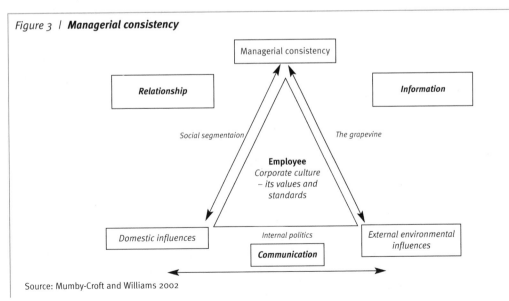

Figure 3 | *Managerial consistency*

Source: Mumby-Croft and Williams 2002

There is a groundswell of evidence pointing to the importance of communication in the organisation and HR's involvement in it, and there exist some models for how we may do this.

COMMUNICATION IS A BROAD SUBJECT

This involvement brings with it a need for understanding. So one of the things that we in HR have to get to grips with is what we mean by communication in the context of the organisation and the HR function. It can be a very broad subject, covered by psychologists, sociologists, business experts, economists and politicians! So the key to success may be to choose those areas on which the HR professional wants to focus his or her efforts rather than having too broad a sweep of the subject.

It used to be impossible to attend a management course without the issue of communication being raised as *the* main blocker for organisational success. This usually occurred during brainstorming sessions with bundles of yellow 'Post-its'® with the word 'communication' littered on the 'threats' quadrant of the flipchart. Likewise, any form of staff survey would raise communication as an issue. ('Management doesn't tell us what's going on,' to paraphrase this sentiment.) Usually the answers to these generalisations didn't get very far!

The past few years have seen a renewed interest in the subject which, given the changes that have taken place, shouldn't be too surprising. The command-and-control days of management are gone. Today's organisations are run by multi- and cross-functional teams in which baby-boomers and Generation-X managers 'show little tolerance for unquestioned authority'. To deal with this situation, the art of persuasion is necessary. This 'involves careful preparation, the proper framing of arguments, the presentation of vivid supporting evidence, and the effort to find the correct emotional match with your audience' (Conger 1998).

This match means that it is not enough for communication to be a one-way ticket (Torrington and Hall 1991). There has to be downward and upward communication. Effective downward communication allows decisions taken by the management of the organisation to be converted into action by employees. Furthermore, it allows for a consistency of action, and it may stimulate a greater commitment on the part of employees. Upward communication helps managers to understand both business and personal issues that affect employees. These are very important reasons for organisations to strive to be excellent in their communication processes and, most importantly, for HR to have a vested interest. So HR professionals have to get to grips with communication with both internal and external stakeholders. Communication has been the underrated competence of the HR professional. It is no longer possible for it to stay as such.

PUTTING HR IN THE MIDDLE OF THE ACTION

So how is all this change affecting the HR profession? An HR director recently said to me, 'I'll know I've been successful when the HR function no longer exists.' It wasn't the first time I'd heard this flawed and rather nonsensical argument. I've never been able to follow the logic and have often wondered at what point HR became so self-deprecatory. Surely the argument should be, 'I'll know HR have been successful when managers demand more and more of our professional services.' One of these services will be the ability to provide tools and techniques that give effective communication and employee engagement.

Working in HR was once like being an uninvited visitor at someone else's party: tolerated but not always welcome. But we've come a long way in the past five years. This is in response to a whole new set of competitive and social forces. In the commercial world 'faster, cheaper, ubiquitous access to information' has created new opportunities and threats. This has had organisational implications, human capital implications and, most importantly, forced HR departments to some new imperatives – organisational development and talent management for the organisation, and outsourcing and cost reduction for itself (Corporate Leadership Council 1999).

So we've fought the talent war, built our defences around operational shared services and have our sights on the lofty heights of the board. Some would say that we are like Icarus ascending, flying closer to the sun with each strategic intervention. But others may argue that we aren't like that at all. Rather, unlike Icarus, we have made sure that we won't crash-land because we've learned how to fly! We've done this through some pretty fundamental re-engineering. First, by making sure that all of our knowledge and understanding is capable of withstanding the new environment into which we have flown. In English this means making sure that we know about strategy, can convert this into HR activity and can communicate it very well. To quote Jack Welch, when speaking about the HR function at the Ninth Human Resource World Congress in Mexico City, 'You've got to put yourself in the middle of the action' (*HR News* July 2002).

We need to become communication experts because, first and foremost, there is a change in the nature of the working relationship. Traditional loyalties went unsaid on the part of employer and employee. But these have now been ploughed into the field of change, leaving a confusing and ill-defined set of relationships. The psychological contract that existed between employer and employee has been transformed into something that feels ephemeral. And yet the need to engage employees has probably never been greater: engaging in change, in the achievement of competitive advantage, in new ways of working, in empowerment and most of all in advocacy of the organisation's products and services, whether these are public or private. To do so means having an approach to communication that goes way beyond that which came before. It means that those in HR have to have communication and 'engagement' strategies and practices that are unprecedented in the profession. The reality is that such skills are only now being recognised.

The second important facet of communication is the need to secure the buy-in of the board and senior management of the organisation as regards HR strategy, policy and even budgetary proposals. These require communication skills that were not necessary when HR investment was seen as an act of faith. HR professionals need the skill and wit that go with the art of persuasion. Understanding how to persuade and engage boards of directors is now an essential part of the role of HR as they compete for scarce resources against a wide range of other professional demands (finance, marketing and so on) and organisational projects. As organisations become more sophisticated in how they prioritise resource allocation, HR must be able to communicate their case excellently.

Finally, the need to 'join up' HR itself as it proposes more sophisticated solutions to increasingly complex problems is again a subject where more effective internal communication could add value.

HR'S INVOLVEMENT IN ORGANISATIONAL COMMUNICATION IS NOW A PRIORITY

These are compelling reasons for anyone in HR to take an interest in the development of communication as a discipline, as a value-added contribution and a core competence of the professional. Anything less will fail to recognise the importance. But what are the drivers for this urgent view?

It's pretty safe to assume that the role of the HR professional is being transformed as we speak. Gone are the days of passive transactional processing. Gone are the days of HR being second stringers to areas that are seen as more business-focused. And gone are the days of HR as a receptacle for the meek and mild. Today's HR professional is a professionally qualified specialist in the way that human resources can be deployed, retained and motivated to achieve the organisation's chosen strategy. The HR function is at the heart of both organisational change and communication. There's a revolution going on in HR. The changing role of the HR professional, which now includes such activities as board-level strategy-setting, change and knowledge management, organisation development and advanced technical interventions (through reward, ER and learning systems), means that a new range of skills is needed to complement those traditionally associated with the function. Combine the revolution in HR and the revolution in communication and there is a convergence of forces that are now on the organisation's agenda. Those in HR will be expected to become expert in the people side of communication in addition to their other roles. This is happening already, and the demand for HR intervention in several levels of communication will grow.

Effective communication for the HR professional will require a refinement of the knowledge, skills, attitudes and behaviours that have been necessary to date. Furthermore, it will require the preparation of an HR communication strategy and plan. In Chapter 6 we shall look at the importance of an HR communication strategy. Figure 4 shows the process that may be used in preparing this. Having agreed a strategy for communication, it will be necessary to detail how this is developed for implementation. An HR communication plan may be the way in which the deployment of resources is achieved, and this is discussed in Chapter 7. Figure 5 shows a proposed schematic for the development of such a plan.

These two diagrams provide the framework against which strategy and plans for communication can be evaluated. But we've still to decide what the precise reason is for all this sudden interest in communication on the part of HR. Why is it that HR is taking on this challenging role?

Figure 4 | **Developing an HR communications plan**

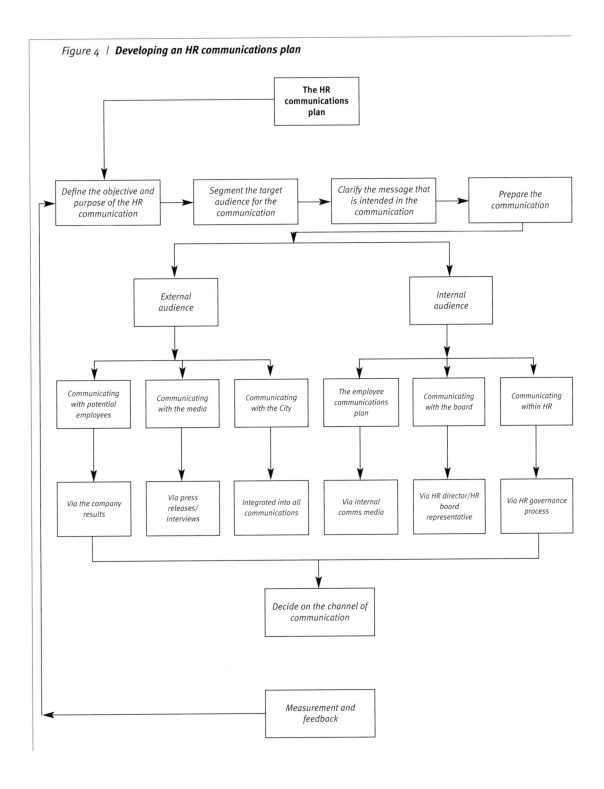

Figure 5 | *Developing an HR communication strategy*

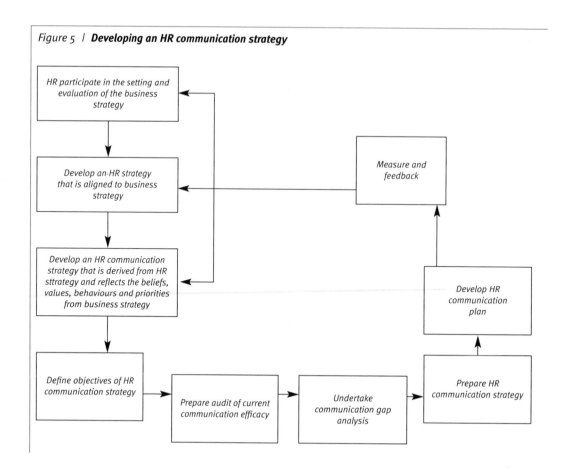

2

The changing role of HR – a communication responsibility

You want the moon? Just say the word and I'll throw a lasso around it. It's a Wonderful Life (1946)

INTRODUCTION

It's easy to say that HR should have a greater responsibility for communication. After all, the function has taken on (*inter alia*) quality, sports and social, and a range of other duties that, important though they may be, don't fit readily into (say) marketing, finance or procurement. In other words HR has been a repository for business functions with a people element that are not strictly 'HR'. Well, at least that used to be so – before the days of human capital, business partnering, shared services and the greater demand on the part of the CEO for high-grade HR. The ante has been well and truly upped. So we have to focus on our core competencies. It is the contention of this book that one of these is now communication.

HR's role in organisational communication should become clear when there is consensus about HR's role in the wider organisational context. This apparently straightforward objective is clouded, though, with the fog of confusion. The matter of role clarity for HR continues to attract a great deal of debate about efficacy, position in the organisation and future direction. There has been a good deal written on this subject, and it has been discussed at length – so much so that John Purcell was recently moved to write:

> *Sometimes debates on the role and position of the HR department or the HR professional become a mixture of guilt and boredom: guilt because of the inevitability of the accusation of limited influence and a function unable to hold its own in the corporate corridors of power; boredom as the seemingly endless debate continues on whether HRM is different from personnel management and whether it matters.* Purcell 2001

Nonetheless it is worth putting a stake in the ground about where we do have agreement. Without this we shall be forever confined to the barracks of non-strategy when we should really be at the heart of key decisions. In fact HR has a very clear role that is fundamental to the success of the organisation. To quote Geoff Armstrong, CIPD Director General, HR people are 'uniquely placed' to design and operate organisations and practices that can lead to success. Understanding this and delivering solutions to the people needs of the organisation is the starting point for positioning HR's role in the communication process.

So this book deals with an important question: 'What should I do about organisational communication if I work in HR?' This question does not only apply to commercial organisations. It is equally important to the HR professional in the public sector where communication is no less challenging, and is often more so. Such a question was peripheral to the HR professional until relatively recently. But times have changed. It is now a core part of the role of those in HR to be able to answer this question with knowledge, understanding and a good grounding in the principles and practice of organisational communication. Why is this?

FORCES DIRECTING HR TO A GREATER INVOLVEMENT IN COMMUNICATION

An obvious reason, touched on earlier, is that the environment within which HR professionals work has changed. In particular, organisations are not the clearly delineated entities that they once were. Technological changes have created opportunities to develop value-adding competitive strategies and also new organisational constructs (sometimes with the prefix 'virtual' attached). On the demand side, globalisation has created bigger markets in which to exploit this advantage. Add in demographic and new social attitudes, and we have an environment at work that is sometimes exciting, sometimes confusing, certainly dynamic and almost always complex. Organisational communication of any sort requires an added professionalism. But when it concerns people, it requires a depth of understanding and a fresh approach. The HR professional can provide this.

But first, what is the context within which HR operates in the contemporary organisation?

Such factors as the changing nature of the workforce have had a real impact on HR's role in the organisation. This has not been the only factor. There are many more. We can start with the new or knowledge economy. It's been written that 'the real measure of any organisation – of any team, any business unit, any company – is not "What products do you sell?" or "How much money do you make?" It's "What ideas do you stand for?"' (*Fast Company* September 2000). Now this particular brand of new economy philosophy may be enlightening to some but bemusing to others. Those free-thinking West Coasters, fired by the venture capital of a dot.com generation and striving for a new set of business principles, would relish a values-based organisation in which creativity and empowerment go hand in hand. But those organisations whose shares have fallen because they failed to persuade the City that they *did* make money and *did* have a decent competitive product portfolio would probably take issue. For them, cost reduction and tight processes are probably the business priorities. And therein lies a dilemma for our particularly turbulent economy.

Those who work in HR have to be able to deal with any of these scenarios. We are constantly reminded of the forces that impinge on organisations. These can affect products or cash flow or profitability or, yes, even the values of the organisation. But we are all grasping to know which of these will have the most impact. Should the organisation tighten up or let go? Trying to forecast this taxes the mind of most chief executives. Yet it is as important for those in HR as for any other function. Our priorities will be to a large extent determined by the forces that affect the organisation and the strategies that are used to compete in this context. Our response to communication is in part influenced by these forces.

There are some particularly important forces changing the demand on HR and the competences with which to work in HR.

The importance of people management

Two recent CIPD reports underline the importance of people management to the modern organisation. The first, *Effective People Management* (CIPD 2000), highlighted the large body of research that had demonstrated a link between human resource management (HRM) and organisational performance, and noted that in the event of a distinctive approach to people management having a marked impact on corporate performance, it must be taken seriously. The work of Dave Ulrich and others has steered a course for HR. It's clear from casual dialogue with other HR professionals that the concept 'strategic business partnering' and its implications has moved into the mainstream of the function. Furthermore, the role of HR professionals as change agents, as 'architects' of people strategy (Gratton, Hope-Hailey, Stiles and Truss 1999), as people champions, as transformers of organisations is one that is increasingly recognised. This has a significant impact on the role of the HR professional who has an obligation to ensure that his or her organisation both understands the impact of good people management and undertakes activity to ensure that it is effective. The second report, *Voices from the Boardroom* (CIPD 2001a), highlighted the fact that the sheer complexity of people management meant that there was 'as yet limited action within organisations attributable to a real understanding of the way the performance/practice link operates'. There is clearly a good deal of work for those of us who have HR as our chosen profession.

Conventional wisdom about HR now tends to focus on the need to close the 'gap between rhetoric and reality' (Gratton *et al* 1999). In practice this means making HR interventions that are strategic, ie aligned to business strategy and with board-level support, as well as operationally excellent. More than anyone in the sphere of HR, David Ulrich has articulated a new HR paradigm that visualises an HR professional who will 'speak with a more confident voice within the organisation. HR's role has to be one of consultancy, co-ordination and maintaining fairness' (Ulrich 1998).

Table 1 | Key HR deliverables and activities

Role/cell	Deliverable/outcome	Metaphor	Activity
Management of strategic human resources	*Executing strategy*	*Strategic partner*	*Aligning HR and business strategy: organisational diagnosis*
Management of firm infrastructure	*Building an efficient infrastructure*	*Administrative expert*	*Re-engineering organisation processes: shared services*
Management of employee contribution	*Increasing employee commitment and capability*	*Employee champion*	*Listening and responding to employees: providing resources to employees*
Management of transformation and change	*Creating a renewed organisation*	*Change agent*	*Managing transformation and change: ensuring capacity for change*

Source: Ulrich 1996

So there is evidence to show the link between HRM and human performance. Those organisations that put effort into developing people 'advantage' will develop competitive advantage. It's as straightforward as that. However, what is not straightforward is engaging the people into this particular framework. Indeed, employee engagement is one of the most difficult tasks facing the modern organisation. Communication will not provide all the answers to this. But it will support a progressive and enlightened HR strategy. HR communication is therefore a key plank for building competitive advantage. The type of intervention and communication to ensure the linkages is shown in Table 1. This is based on the CIPD model about the effectiveness of people management. Onto this has been transposed the type of communication intervention that might be relevant. Communication is a strategic issue. HR's involvement is too.

The impact of technology on HR

The other great outstanding issue for HR has been its use of technology. 'Computers have been transformed into information technology and then into information and communications technology. This is a fundamental shift in terms of what technology can do' (Hartley and Bruckmann 2002). Underinvestment in HR systems was a feature of organisational life for the function. However, there is evidence that this is changing. A Corporate Leadership Council study noted that enterprise resource planning (ERP) systems had been deployed in the majority of large corporations in the USA and that HR applications were 'among the most widely adopted ERP modules across corporations' (Corporate Leadership Council 1999). HR functions had moved beyond ERP solutions and were beginning to use the Web more aggressively. Such a trend is taking hold in the UK as well, and the application of technology in HR in UK organisations is increasing.

There are now solutions to the banes of the life of the HR professional: lack of recognition at strategic level and lack of decent technology to deal with the transactions of HR. There is now no excuse for those who work in HR to be exclusively the provider of the nuts and bolts of people management. But operational matters remain important, of course. Without excellence in these areas HR will not be accepted at the higher level of strategy. But HR is now expected to deliver these through technology, where possible, and focus the bulk of its professional attention on enabling the organisation to achieve sustained success through effective people strategy and practice.

This is not to underestimate the challenge of getting HR onto the strategic agenda of organisations. The presence of the HR director on the board is still an issue to be addressed (though the debate about it is becoming somewhat tired). The thing that will help to deal with the issue will be a pincer movement of pressures from within the HR function itself and, as importantly, from the chief executive, who will demand strategic HR as part of an integrated set of measures to contribute towards competitive advantage or sustained business success.

Let's assume that the organisation is HR-partnered, has HR technology, has a strategy and has embraced the importance of effective people management as a key contributor to competitive advantage. What a great platform this would be! But would it be enough? The answer is probably no. There is an extra ingredient of the success recipe that is needed: effective communication. It will be no use having the vehicle for delivering people excellence if decision-makers don't know about it (the board), those who will benefit from its use don't know about it (employees and potential employees) and those who invest in organisations don't see it as a key for success (the City, shareholders and government). So communicating effective people management and practice will be as important as having the practice in the first place. Moreover, the job of communicating people issues will fall increasingly to the HR professional. If this is the case, then a greater understanding of communication in the organisation and how to make it effective will be an essential competence of the HR professional.

SO WHAT IS THE NEWLY DEFINED ROLE FOR HR?

The single most powerful conclusion we can make about the organisational context for people management is that whereas 'operational and technical excellence is fundamental to ensuring customers are delighted repeatedly ... hard evidence confirms that success only comes from people' (CIPD 2001). These are Geoff Armstrong's words, and they are increasingly resonant in the boardrooms (and back offices) of the organisation. Given the recognition that people are *the* key to delivering sustained success for the organisation, the potential sphere of influence for HR is in the area of greatest added value. People issues are at the fore, and workable solutions to complex people challenges are vital. It is a prime role for HR to come up with these solutions.

So there it is. The baton has been passed on. We can't ask for any more. But how do we then grasp the baton? One way is for us to make sure we understand the forces at work in the organisation, can deal and work with those forces and ultimately support the organisation's quest for a sustained competitive position in the face of them. To do this demands excellence on the part of HR professionals.

Such a dynamic requires a response that goes well beyond the traditional boundaries associated with personnel and training. It requires a paradigm shift in the way the profession interfaces with its organisation. Are there things upon which we can agree in defining the role of HR to deal with these new challenges?

THE EVOLUTION OF HR

The first thing we can conclude is that there are more professionals working in HR in the year 2003 than at any other time in the history of the profession. From a membership of 34 in 1913, growing to about 800 in 1939 (Leopold 2002), the professional body of personnel and development now has over 115,000 members in the UK. Given the arguments that have raged about the role of HR, this growth is remarkable. Furthermore, given the tight focus on the costs of support in most organisations, the fact that so many HR professionals are employed is perhaps a testament to the value placed on the role by organisations.

The increase in numbers employed in the profession is one thing, but there has also been a broadening of the scope of the HR professional. Contrast the following two descriptions of personnel and HRM. The core text of the personnel manager for many years was Pigors and Myers's book, *Personnel Administration* (1969 edition). Written in the 1940s, it was still a standard reference work for the personnel professional as late as the 1970s. In it the authors note that:

> *the newly designated personnel administrator cannot by himself solve personnel problems. He is no miracle worker. Rather he is an advisor to line or operating management on personnel*

problems and an exponent of a point of view and methods designed to help management in getting effective results with people. Pigors and Myers 1969

Some would still relate to this today. But contrast it with a recent viewpoint:

At the centre of many HRM approaches to organisational transformation and culture change is the concept of the personnel or HR professional as change agent . . . the change agent role has grown in significance and complexity. To partly capture these changes, a new four-fold typology of HR change agent roles is proposed: champions, adapters, consultants and synergists. Caldwell 2001

We may conclude from these two works separated by 50 years that HR professionals have moved from being only administrators to change agents as well.

So the HR profession has come a long way since Peter Drucker's indictment of the personnel manager's role as 'partly a file clerk's job, partly a social worker's job and partly fire-fighting to head off union trouble or settle it' (Donkin 2001). The benefits of having excellent people management in an organisation are now well documented. The CIPD has articulated the case in *The Change Agenda* that progressive HR practices can significantly enhance company performance, can lead to higher levels of commitment amongst employees and can lead to a better transfer and use of knowledge in a knowledge economy (CIPD 2001).

HR BEYOND ITS TRADITIONAL BOUNDARIES

It is absolutely right that those who work in HR should become more strategic. This is because organisations will need to have people management as a core competence if they are to achieve sustained competitive or service success. How they get there will be by having switched-on HR professionals who are able to leverage their knowledge of people issues into action that is both organisation-wide and sustainable over the long term – ie strategic HR.

The tools for achieving excellent people management are now documented and proven. In their comprehensive presentation of the *HR Scorecard*, Becker, Huselid and Ulrich noted that 'new opportunities for HR professionals, new demands for HR's accountability, and new perspectives on measuring organisational performance have all converged', resulting in a new approach to managing the organisation's 'HR architecture' (Becker, Huselid and Ulrich 2001). This convergence has been most fortuitous, giving HR, possibly for the first time in its illustrious history, the business case *and* the business methodology. We are awash with evidence.

HR now has its own champions and gurus who have articulated not only the reasons for which organisations should have HR skills but also the roles that they might play. In his many works on the role of HR, Ulrich has confirmed the new responsibilities of HR professionals. He has articulated four key areas: strategic partner, administrative expert, employee champion and change agent. The deliverables associated with these roles are shown in Figure 6. This approach has become the new norm for HR functions around the world. In the diagram Ulrich describes the various roles of HR as the function delivers a new agenda that is simultaneously strategic and operational:

- HR professionals act as business partners ensuring that HR strategy and business strategy are aligned.

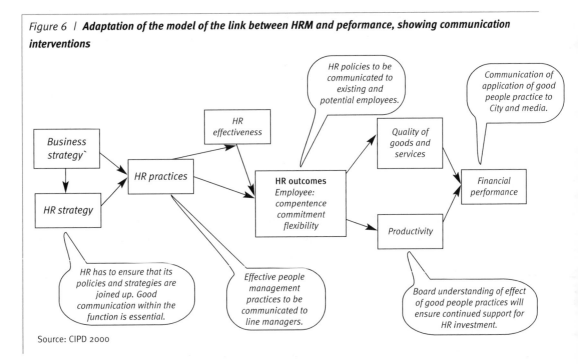

*Figure 6 | **Adaptation of the model of the link between HRM and peformance, showing communication interventions***

Source: CIPD 2000

- They also deliver operational excellence through an efficient (often technology-based) infrastructure that streamlines HR transactional work.

- At the same time, HR professionals act as employee champion by developing solutions to employee needs as they go about their work.

- HR professionals become the change agent and expert, acting as transformers of organisations through great people strategies and plans.

Ulrich's perspective has itself been transformational and has provided a new impetus to the role of the HR professional.

THE CORE ELEMENTS OF THE HR FUNCTION

The types of activity and responsibility of those who work in HR are many and varied. However, it is perhaps useful to try to synthesise these into their core components. In the post-Ulrich world, it may be possible to see HR as comprising two core elements:

- *Strategic business partner.* In practice, this means that each part of the organisation – such as a division, a business unit or a department – will 'own' very little by way of HR resources. Instead it will have a strategic business partner whose role will be to provide a two-way channel of strategic information and advice. In the first instance, the HR business partner is primarily a 'people strategist'. He or she will work with the board or senior management team of the organisation to make sure that people implications of strategic decisions are taken into account at the highest level. The second part of the role will be to ensure that sufficient HR professional resources are provided from a shared service of HR resources to ensure that the organisation is able to deal with people changes effectively. This role will also include HR policy-setting.

- *HR shared services*. Whereas each division or part of the organisation used to have its own specific HR resource covering its unique needs, nowadays the trend is towards sharing HR resources. This allows a much better demand and supply match. Peaks and troughs in activity and variations in skill requirements can be met in a much better way. An added benefit is that better terms can be obtained from external suppliers of HR services – a growing part of the HR armoury.

It is of course essential that these two core components converge into a coherent, end-to-end service of policy, strategy, stewardship and supply, so that HR offers joined-up solutions. It is no longer enough to have a reward strategy independent of an employee relations strategy that is itself independent of training and development. There needs to be this joining-up because the organisation demands such a view. HR decisions will also be based on a consistent set of management information for the HR function, whether this is about staff attitudes, cost of service or legislative changes.

Running through both elements is a greater emphasis on HR's role in organisational communication. Indeed, a recent study concluded that:

> *HR professionals are increasingly taking responsibility for corporate internal communication functions ... The survey of 100 leading companies found that in 38% of cases the head of internal communications reported to the HR Director. This was up from 20% in 2000.* People Management 8 August 2002

We can speculate on the reasons for this. But the prime one is recognition that communication and people management can no longer be treated as separate activities. The effectiveness of one is dependent on the effectiveness of the other, and combining both into a single management process is a logical conclusion. In some instances this means combining the role of HR with that of communication. In others it means a greater co-ordination and co-operation among those responsible for both activities. But overall we may conclude that HR's role in the management of change will bring with it the need for an understanding of communication and the techniques that make for its success. How might this occur?

THE IMPORTANCE OF COMMUNICATION FOR HR BUSINESS PARTNERS

One of the prime responsibilities of the HR business partner will be to make sure that all the people aspects of his or her organisation's business strategy are taken care of: that the HR strategy is aligned with the business strategy. Then he or she has to make sure that those HR services necessary to deliver it are in place on time, to specification and within budget.

Fine. But imagine a scenario where all this is understood within the HR community but nowhere else – where the HR business partner has failed to communicate the outcomes of the HR deliberations to any of the key stakeholders.

Well, in the first instance we know that organisations will fail to deliver their strategy if certain criteria have not been satisfied. Bragg (1996) has listed some of the reasons for these failures. Amongst the reasons cited for parts of an organisation not getting the decisions it wants are:

- a failure to take the audience with you
- wrongly assuming that the key players all share identical goals
- ignoring emotional reactions to proposals
- forgetting that men and women are irrational
- trying too hard
- having no knowledge of others' hidden agendas
- underestimating the political dimensions of organisational life.

These points should resonate with anyone who has had an HR policy go wrong, failed to communicate adequately before launching a new service or got nowhere with the board. So it has to be a key part of the role of the HR business partner to make sure that engagement has taken place in all the right areas.

A further point is that 'one of the most significant and undervalued managerial skills is the ability to influence others' (Bragg 1996). This adage applies to HR skills as much as any other aspect of management. Key to our success is honing these influencing skills to the point where we have them as powerful weapons in the HR armoury. HR communication is one facet of this influencing competence. Proficiency in HR communication will alleviate some of the symptoms of poor influencing.

THE IMPORTANCE OF COMMUNICATION TO THOSE WORKING IN HR SHARED SERVICES

It is clear to see that the HR business partners need to be on the ball with their communication contribution to the effective implementation of HR strategy. But this responsibility is not just confined to them. Those HR professionals (a growing number) who are part of the shared-services model of HR should equally have concern with communications and the competence to make it work effectively.

Shared services in this context means the following:

- personnel services such as absence management, discipline and grievance
- recruitment
- learning, training and development
- employee relations
- reward.

Given that communication forms such an important part of the delivery of these services, it may be that HR communication itself is an HR shared service.

SCENARIOS FOR HR COMMUNICATION

The principle of ensuring effective communication to key stakeholders is as important in these functions as it is in any other area of HR. So it is worth looking at the type of scenario that would make the issue of communication important to those who work in HR shared services.

- There has been an increase in absence caused by a significant change programme being undertaken by the company. As a result, investment has been made in a new 'well-being' scheme. Communicating the benefits of this scheme, how it will work, the relative roles of line managers and HR and so on will be a vital part of the roll-out of the scheme. This will require the following communication actions:

  - gaining board-level approval for the investment, because it competes with other investments the organisation may be considering
  - gaining agreement within the HR community that the scheme is right for employee relations and reward representatives
  - communicating and gaining the agreement of the employee representatives
  - communicating with line managers how they should operate the scheme
  - communicating with employees the details and procedures involved in taking advantage of the scheme.

  Each of these actions will require communications expertise to varying degrees.

- The opening of a new call centre requires a significant level of recruitment in a particular geographic area. The recruitment team will have to make sure that:

  - they have a recruitment strategy and that this is communicated to the managers involved in opening the call centre
  - they have a sufficiently attractive package to offer potential employees and that this is understood in the open market through an external marketing campaign
  - the organisation is recognised as an attractive employer – probably through the development and communication of an employer brand.

  In this example the emphasis is likely to be on both external and internal communications, and those in HR responsible for recruitment will have to be proficient in this type of external marketing approach.

So for those who are in the HR shared-services area, the use of effective communications is as important as that for HR business partners.

HOW CAN HR IMPROVE THE COMMUNICATION CONTRIBUTION TO THE ORGANISATION?

The case for the HR professional as a communication facilitator is a strong one. However, the increased profile of this facet of the role means that we shall have to be more proactive in the area than perhaps we have been in the past. There are some basic things that the HR professional will have to do if he or she is to make this new, greater contribution to the communication effectiveness of the organisation. In subsequent chapters this argument will be developed further. In the meantime here are some of the activities that may enhance this important part of the job:

- *Understanding the 'audiences' or 'publics' for HR communications*. A principle to bear in mind here is that communications have to be adapted to meet the needs of different audiences. Understanding who the audiences are and delivering appropriate solutions is known in marketing terms as segmentation, targeting and positioning. The target group is broken down into homogenous segments and specific communications are designed for them. Examples of the audiences include the board, senior managers, employees, potential employees and so on.

- *Understanding the tools and techniques for communications*. Given that the staff notice is no longer the single vehicle by which communications are distributed, those in HR will have to know better what other tools and techniques are available for their use. Is there a corporate intranet, for example? How are team briefings used?

- *Understanding the best methods of obtaining feedback from the communication*. It is no longer enough to have a one-way flow. The success of communication will be dependent upon a proactive two-way flow of information.

In addition, the development of communication skills is an imperative.

CONCLUSION: HR'S COMMUNICATION ROLE

The previous narrative was intended as a summary of how HR's role has changed and continues to change. HR professionals now have a much more strategic part to play in the organisation's function. They still have responsibility for those things rather disparagingly described as 'trans-actional', as though they weren't important (you know, like paying people on time!), but there has been a conceptual shift in the type of work in which they are involved. Nowadays HR professionals will be expected to advise on the business strategy, just as any other high-level professional would.

However, there is also a recognition it is not enough merely to be able to identify the strategy for people to be aligned with the business strategy: the HR professional also has to make it work. To do so requires the engagement of a wide range of stakeholders. These are external (the community, the City and the media) and internal (the employees, the board and colleagues within HR). A key part of this new role is the ability to communicate in a way that secures 'buy-in' from the stakeholders. This is more than the cascade of the message. It is full-on, pro-fessional communication of a type that has rarely been seen and only occasionally been used. The HR professional now has a role in areas as clear-cut as staff communication and as woolly as 'spin'. The latter will be particularly difficult, given the political neutrality of the function.

But what does communication actually mean? The next two chapters try to offer some definitions of the subject in its broadest sense and in its organisational context.

3

Forces for change – factors making communication a new priority for HR

Toto, I've a feeling we're not in Kansas any more. The Wizard of Oz (1939)

According to the dictionary, communication is:

> *The imparting or exchange of ideas, information and feelings.*

Many companies focus on the 'imparting' and tend to overlook the 'exchange' aspect. If communication is to be successful in a business context, both elements have an important role to play.

Poor communication can cause a business to fail – whether through a breakdown of understanding between directors and shareholders, managers and employees, or a company and its customers.

Where a company leaves a vacuum of information, then someone will fill it with rumour, innuendo or guesswork. Wasted energy, poor use of resources and chaos for the business are the likely results.

Whilst many companies spend millions on external communication, far less investment is made – either intellectual or financial – in communicating with those at the heart of the business: the employees. Businesses are operating in a fast-paced environment where information is exchanged in unprecedented volumes and at speed. Most workforces are now more diverse, mobile and sophisticated in terms of their expectations. Effective communication is vital in harnessing their energy, commitment and ideas. The kind of employee we all want in our businesses expects to understand the business objectives and to be consulted and involved in moving the business forward.

Business leaders need to make sure that their organisation has a coherent communication framework in place to meet employee expectations. Although it is unfortunately a cliché to say it, good employee communication does start with the company vision. But it's a mistake to think of this as some ethereal, fuzzy concept that is detached from the real, day-to-day business. The vision and values that are established within a business should add clarity and rigour to business thinking and decision-making. They should provide employees with a broad guide for day-to-day actions. The exact words used to articulate the vision are very important, and it's worth spending some time getting them right. The challenges being set need to inspire and capture the imaginations of employees at all levels and be readily understood and remembered. 'Market-testing' your vision statement before publishing it widely is always a good idea.

Once the ethos and organisational purpose have been established, the communication channels that traditionally have fallen within the remit of the HR professional can be used to best effect. HR has a critical role to play in maintaining the consistency, coherence and integrity of the organisational 'dialogue'.

Recruitment processes, induction, and training and development programmes are all powerful ways of communicating the company philosophy. How an organisation rewards its people, the benefit choices offered and the way success is recognised say so much about what the business wants to achieve.

The performance management framework establishing targets for teams and individuals must be managed in such a way as to reinforce the company ethos. Annual partnership agreements where goals and training needs are agreed rather than imposed make appraisals an opportunity to exchange feedback and ideas for improving the business rather than a one-way feedback session.

However it is approached, keeping the lines of communication open between employer and employee is vital to the long-term health of an organisation. Businesses can enrich their planning processes by involving a broad cross-section of the workforce, publishing plans widely and encouraging feedback. There is no monopoly on wisdom at board level, and you can be sure that front-line employees will have reflected long and deeply on issues affecting their role and their customers.

Businesses can really benefit from canvassing employee opinions with formal surveys – asking questions on a whole range of operational issues, not just the obvious 'employee satisfaction'. Informal methods of gathering anecdotal feedback can also be very useful.

There is every chance today of establishing a fruitful and highly productive dialogue within business if the range of technology available is used and HR professionals work with business leaders to manage a coherent internal communications strategy. Bruce Thew, Chief Executive, Ceridien Europe

INTRODUCTION

We've seen how the development of HR's role has led to a dramatic shift in priorities. Strategic business partnering, effective policy-making and the evolution of the shared services model have transformed the way in which HR operates. One of the important things in this new area of responsibility is to understand what factors, both external and internal, are likely to have an effect on communication within the organisation. The reason for doing this is so that HR communication strategy takes account of all the forces in play. In fact, this is like any other strategy-setting process.

The first step is to gather information about the environment in which we operate. In describing the BT Global Challenge Round the World Yacht Race 1996–7, Walters noted that one of the critical success factors for winning was, in one case at least, 'adherence to a strict policy of comprehensive information search before making a strategic decision' (Walters, Mackie and Bacon 1997). This would seem to be a good maxim for strategic decisions. Of course, some would disagree with this principle on the assumption that comprehensive information is often difficult to get in today's uncertain society. Nonetheless it is worth the effort to understand what is going on around us when making decisions about organisational strategy, even if the results are less than perfect. This is also true when trying to decide on an organisation's communication strategy. What things are in play that might affect how and when we decide to communicate? Understanding the context in which an organisation is operating is, in fact, an essential part of the communicator's art, even if sometimes it can be unhelpful (and at other times disastrous – an intelligent and highly qualified individual wanting to 'bury bad news' under worse news, for example?).

FACTORS AFFECTING ORGANISATIONAL COMMUNICATION: EXTERNAL AND INTERNAL

If an HR professional were to list the factors that have triggered an organisational communication during the past five to ten years it is likely that the following would appear:

- *External*
  - European social legislation
  - Change of government
  - Economic boom and bust
  - September 11
  - Take-over or merger
  - Demographic change
  - The talent war and recruitment problems
- *Internal*
  - Reorganisation
  - New MD/CEO
  - Retention problems
  - Marketing and advertising activity
  - Opening or closure of business units
  - Pay and reward

Make your own list and see how many issues need both information and communication from within the HR function. In fact the list looks to be a snapshot of near-term economic and social history. There are other, more sophisticated ways of collating this list. Try PEST, SWOT, five-forces analysis or any one of a number of excellent approaches. Table 2 shows seven trends forecast for tomorrow's workplace that demonstrate the radical possibility for change now facing us. This analysis sees a range of economic variables – not only the new economy but a

*Table 2 | **Tomorrow's workplace – seven trends***

1 The **new** economy – faster growth, new jobs, old jobs transformed
2 The **relationship** economy – interpersonal relationships will be more important to work
3 The **fulfilment** economy – jobs will become more fulfilling – and more stressful
4 The **all-age** economy – work will start sooner in life and finish later
5 The **outsourced** workplace – outsourcing will enter a new radical phase
6 The **self-managed** workplace – people will manage their own work
7 The **consumerist** workplace – consumer values will invade work

Source: Moynagh and Worsley 2001

more inclusive, relationship-based version – combining with a mix of 'work models'. Combinations of these will produce a workplace very different from the one we know.

We can see that these forces are both external and internal. Understanding them will be an important part of the critical path to effective communication. This kind of conclusion is as important to the business strategist as it is to the finance specialist, to the marketer as it is to the technologist. It is equally important to the HR professional in his or her role as policy-maker and business partner.

This chapter will identify some of these forces and their implications for organisational communication. It is important to recognise these as influences on the communication process and practice. A voice in the pattern, structure and nature of work is becoming increasingly necessary if the work is to be delivered as required. Communication forms an increasingly important part of this process. What these forces have produced is a change in culture and a new paradigm for organisations. Combined, they are powerful and critical success factors. They can no longer be marginalised in the HR decision-making and communication process. The following sections will look at these in more detail.

It is possible to identify several areas in which massive and fundamental change is happening that affects the effectiveness or otherwise of organisational communication.

A media-based society and its effect on communication expectations

We live in a media-aware age, where scores of sound-bites are presented to us daily by the media channels. Compare the traditional staff notice with the headlines and sub-headlines of the *Daily Mail* or *Daily Mirror*. Compare the traditional job advertisement with any website, that has to grab attention immediately because lost business is a click away. These give some idea of the new media and its effect on expectations. Furthermore, there is a view that 'because the media are seen as objective, the public will more readily accept their "version" than the company's own public relations materials' (Rouse and Rouse 2002). This is a powerful force and one that affects almost every aspect of an individual's relationship with society.

Take the description of the economic problems encountered by United Airlines late in 2002. In a *New York Times* article there were quotations and views from a customer who was a hockey player, the mayor of Chicago, the governor of Illinois, a political scientist and a manager of a hospital radiology department – a business story seen from a wide variety of views. This is the nature of today's media reporting. If this is the case in our personal lives, ie the stuff we read and hear about outside work, why should organisational life be any different? Won't the stakeholders in the organisation expect to see the way communication takes place outside to be replicated inside the organisation? Or will they be happy to see different strokes for different situations? My money is on the former, which means that HR communication will need to reflect the way in which communication takes place in the press, on TV and through other types of media. We'd better make sure that no one is more than one click away from what we mean by our 'people communication'.

In our knowledge economy, expectations about 'work' have changed and expectations about what information an individual will expect to receive in his or her work have also changed. Futurists such as Don Tapscott, who spoke at the CIPD 2001 Conference at Harrogate, talk of partnerships and freelance work as well as the traditional FTE model of employment. How does communication take place with this diverse workforce? *Funky Business* told us that 'people with access to relevant information are beginning to challenge any type of authority ... [and] total transparency also has a tendency to reveal and expose those not really adding any value' (Nordstrom and Ridderstrale 2000). Greater access to information and the type of information proliferated by a diverse range of media have changed expectations.

These changes demand a different way of engaging those who work for and with organisations. Communication, and more specifically HR communication, is part and parcel of this engagement process. The reality of the influence of the media on organisational communication is now recognised. The real challenge here will be to match organisational needs with employee needs at a time when employee expectations are greater than ever (Arnott 1987). The modern media and its many advantages can provide a vital learning experience for those responsible for communication.

The Internet and new communication channels

A factor that has contributed to increased access to information is the Internet, of which so much has been written. In terms of business structure, the Internet and the growth of everything 'e' have been revolutionary. Notwithstanding the global readjustment after the dot.com 'ex-' and 'implosions', the Web has been a force for transformation and change. Furthermore, the spread of the Internet has made any previous concept of information redundant.

Yet how dramatic has this revolution actually been? We can see from the following statistics that the Internet has been more than a passing phase. The US Department of Commerce has put together information on the amount of time it has taken for critical inventions to reach 50 million users. The following are the results (Sloman 2001):

- Radio   38 years
- PC   16 years
- Television   13 years
- Internet   4 years

Furthermore, its commercial impact has gone beyond previous predictions and is forecast to reach $6.7 billion in 2004, or 13 per cent of world trade. Such statistics probably underestimate the sheer scope of the effect of the Internet on trade and commerce – even less so on the attitudinal change towards communication.

Against this backdrop, it shouldn't be surprising that the issue of communication and the effect on it of the spread of the World Wide Web are critical in considering how communication takes place in the modern organisation.

Let's just put this in context with the make-up of the workforce. How, for example, will Generation Y, the Millennials, born between 1977 and 1997, regard the impact of technology on their own working lives? A recent analysis noted that 'the oldest members of Generation Y grew up with laptops, cell phones and the Internet, and the youngest members may grow up in a world with universal broadband access and fantastic biotechnology discoveries' (*Workplace Visions* No.4 2002). It's difficult to imagine that the prevalence of technology in the lives of this particular segment of the workforce won't have an effect on how they regard communication.

Changes in the nature of work

Internal to the organisation is the massive change that has taken place in the very nature of work and the working environment. Old rules seem less and less relevant. There are new priorities, new power-bases, new mandates. Those who work in organisations are faced with an environment in which complexity and uncertainty are normal, everyday characteristics, in which self-management is as important as being managed. The success of these organisations will come not from adherence to written rules but from flexible application of agreed principles. Organisations cannot be defined in rigid forms. They do not follow one or two familiar patterns. We have matrix and bureaucracy, hierarchy and flat structure.

In spite of the potential in such a scenario, research into this area has shown that organisations have a good way to go before they win hearts and minds. The Gallup Organisation survey results showed that (Buckingham and Wilde 2001):

- more than 80 per cent of employees in the UK were not 'engaged' at work
- employees who are not engaged cost the organisations tens of millions of pounds
- the longer employees stay with an organisation, the less engaged they become
- in many organisations the culture is incoherent.

These results come at a time when the engagement of employees at work is shown as a key differentiator for success. The heat is bound to be on, therefore, to improve this situation, to make sure that employees are fully committed and that competitive advantage can follow. The solution to this is of course a multi-faceted one, but HR communication has a role to play.

An extremely pressing issue in this type of environment is to secure the commitment of a workforce for whom the perception and actuality of work have changed. To engage in this new relationship it has been suggested that:

as more and more divergent values rub shoulders with each other, organisations will have to state explicitly what values are expected of their employees ... Some people will select where they work on the basis of these statements: 'I believe in those values too; I would like to work for them.'
Moynagh and Worsley 2001

One of the most dramatic accompaniments to these competitive developments has been a shift in what we mean by employment. Take this quotation from Richard Donkin:

Something has happened to the way we work. Once there was work, and what we understood as work was what we were paid to be doing. Today there is what we do, and sometimes the benefits to our employer of what we do are unclear. Sometimes it is difficult to think of what we do as work, and sometimes there seems to be so much work to shift that we feel overwhelmed. Once we left our work behind. Today we take it with us with our mobile phones, our pagers and our computers. Our work life is woven, warp across weft, into the texture of our domestic existence. Donkin 2001

Consider the many different types of relationship with the organisation. There are, of course, full-time employees in the traditional sense of the word. Then there are part-time employees. There are full- and part-time agency or temporary workers. There are fixed-term contractors. There are home workers. There are those who are completely peripatetic and whose working day consists of hot desks and laptop mobile communications. There are consultants and advisers. The clover-leaf has opened and one size does not fit all in terms of being an employee. Without wishing to overdramatise, there has been a far-reaching change in the way we employ and are employed.

The challenge of engaging the workforce is greater than ever. It will make the question of how individuals rationalise their working lives a very real issue for the organisation, and the HR professional will have a key role to play in whatever the solution is – which could be a new work ethic that does not always value the prolonged, hard-working life above everything else (Donkin 2001).

If it is indeed true that a new type of mentality is becoming the norm for employment, then the need to engage employees in something that does not look and sound like the old world of work is important. The challenge of communicating with employees assumes increased priority in this environment.

There is evidence to suggest that organisations have recognised the importance of effective communication with employees, but that this has been only partially successful. A major study found that most organisations were in fact communicating their aims to employees but that there was hardly any upward communication. The effect of this, not surprisingly, was that employees didn't feel that the strategy had been communicated *clearly* (Gratton *et al* 1999). The conclusion we may reach is that it is not sufficient to have a communication plan that is one-way. Effective communication is a two-way process.

Corporate governance and the need for better communication

And what about how companies are run? In the post-Maxwell, post-Enron era, the nature of corporate governance has been or is in the process of being transformed. Boards of directors are likely to consist of a powerful mix of full-time and non-executive directors. In some organisations the majority of board members are already non-executive. Shareholders expect to see a board that is both efficient and committed to effective corporate governance. Social and environmental responsibility, better understanding and control of strategic direction and a general demand for more and better information will have an equally profound effect on the organisation.

The way in which the organisation relates to all its stakeholders, including shareholders, the City and the community, is under review or being changed. The way it explains its actions via the media is under scrutiny. The upshot is that the contemporary organisation is likely to be a rich mosaic of different employment and governance patterns but with some common beliefs about fairness, responsibility and ethics. Ensuring that appropriate information is transmitted to the right people in a timely fashion and in a way that can be understood and taken on board is a very real challenge, but it is now something that is rapidly attaining mandatory status.

Organisational culture and communication

A key determinant of how and why the organisation communicates is its corporate culture. Culture has been defined in many ways, although the most famous is probably that of Martin Bower, formerly managing director of McKinsey and Company, whose informal definition was 'the way we do things around here' (Deal and Kennedy 1982). The way in which the culture of the organisation manifests itself is through a variety of overt and covert signals. The mission, vision or values statement is often the most outward commitment. But culture can also be inferred from the physical characteristics of the organisation, from the canteen to the car park. (In one organisation I know there was a real *cachet* about who was first in the car park and right bang in front of the entrance to the building. The MD was always first in. What does this say about the organisation? You decide!) Likewise the stories that abound within and about the organisation are often indicative of what the organisation is actually like, what it would like to be like, and what its employees believe it is like.

Table 3 | *Harrison's model of cultures and structures*

Culture	Structure	Major implications for communication
Role – strong emphasis on defining roles	Bureaucratic hierarchy	This structure suggests that there are very definite 'rules', 'procedures' and 'channels' for communication
Achievement – eg small family business	Family group	Provided the group is working to the same goals, then communication should be direct and effective
Power – held by a few individuals	Web with power source in the middle	The important communication comes from the centre; other messages may be discarded or ignored
Support – members feel personal stake	Equal partnership	The organisation will survive as long as the members maintain their commitment to the ideals and values

Source: After Hartley and Bruckman 2002

One view commonly held is that the culture of the organisation is tied to its structure. Table 3 highlights the issues involved. In this case it is possible to identify the issues for communication of any type of cultural structural relationship.

So what are the guidelines on how communication might be tackled within a particular type of organisational culture? Let's take some examples of appropriate or inappropriate communication for each.

Role culture

In this type of organisation there will be strong culture of defined responsibility. The way we do things around here is generally by the book. Hay points and other grade indicators count for a lot, and there are clear departmental boundaries. In this instance, the mode of communication will have to mirror such rules and procedures if it is to get through. So if we want to communicate about pay there is likely to be a formal process of consultation, cascade communication and line managers passing the message through the hierarchy. Of course, the freethinking HR professional can try to bypass this and use alternative methods. The Web is a great liberator in this respect. But success is not guaranteed, however much the dislike of bureaucracy and admiration of dot.com principles. Knowing what you can get away with is as much a part of successful communication as knowing the alternatives, attractive though they may seem.

Achievement culture

An achievement culture is typical of the small family business or the high-tech start-up. Its participants have the same set of goals and objectives, and communication can be to the point, either formal or informal (it'll get through anyway), and succinct. There is no need for long and wordy explanations, because members of this culture are likely to be 'on message'.

Power culture

In a power culture the central message is the only one that matters. This culture is typified by strong leadership through which all decisions and most communications are channelled. The size of the organisation is not relevant because the principles still hold good. In this culture, effective communication will need the 'sign-off' of the centre or else it will have no credence when it filters through to the recipients.

Support culture

In this type of culture reaffirmation of the beliefs and values of the organisation will be the most critical aspect of communication, because this is at the very heart of its existence. Communication that in any way contradicts any of the basic beliefs is threatening the very existence of the organisation and will be regarded with suspicion.

Organisational culture will play a part in determining how any communication takes place. Recognition of the recipe that is best for the mix of communication and culture is in the domain of the HR professional, whose competence extends into both areas.

Competition for scarce resources in organisations and the need to communicate a 'case'

The prevailing culture of the organisation and its implications for communication is an area to which HR professionals will address themselves with gusto. It's right on our radar. Something that probably hasn't been that much of a turn-on, but that had better be in future, is the business case, ie how do HR communicate the power of their case in the great budget scramble? How can the HR professional raise his or her game to compete in the fight for scarce resources within the organisation? Communication plays a big part in this.

Once, getting the HR budget was straightforward (if not easy). A bid was put to the company's number-crunchers to be tabled along with all of the other bids from within the organisation. HR were asked to reduce theirs by 10 to 15 per cent. Approval was given and one of two things would happen:

- We would be allowed to get on with spending the budget.
- We would be asked to reduce the training budget half-way through the year as our contribution to the six-monthly reforecast.

At the time, this process seemed to be a bit of a drag. After all, we wanted our share of the budget because people were our greatest asset. Nowadays this type of process seems to be a tad amateurish. Why? Because in an organisation where resources are scarce (ie most organisations!) those in HR have to justify their requests for budget in the same way as every other business project. It has to be backed up by the rigour of the business case, has to be seen to be aligned with the business strategy and, of increasing importance, has to be communicated professionally and well to the board or leaders of the organisation.

Resources are no longer given as an act of faith to support functions such as HR. *People Management* carried an article in which it was argued that 'until we understand exactly what value we deliver and are able to communicate this to our colleagues, we will regularly be sidelined' (Alberg 2002). Therefore HR has to be excellent at representing itself at board and senior management level. Communicating with the top management team of the organisation to persuade them of the efficacy of the 'case' for HR is no longer an occasional demand but a basic management task on the part of the HR professional. To quote the US *HR Magazine*, 'once considered a bonus for an HR worker, business literacy will be a prerequisite' (*HR Magazine* July 2002).

A NEW PARADIGM FOR ORGANISATIONS AND THE CHALLENGE TO COMMUNICATION

We may conclude that a new paradigm, pattern or model of the organisation is beginning to emerge, one that shifts away from command and control to a more diverse set of attitudes. Instead of the 'one right way' there will be a variety of ways, which is a natural development of the plurality of the twenty-first century but one that will require an unprecedented level of sophistication in the thinking and methodology behind organisational communication. This will therefore place a real challenge on the shoulders of those whose role it is to come up with intelligible communication, and a far greater emphasis on individualism – with all its implications for the mass-market approach to communication.

In total, these trends (if they do happen) mean that the organisation's approach to communication will have to be something far more sophisticated and holistic than those that preceded. Communicating in a rigid bureaucracy was relatively straightforward. But 'the bureaucratic model is no longer used in many companies, especially among firms that rely on multi-skilled, creative people for their competitive advantage' (Rouse and Rouse 2002). In this type of organisation – perhaps it will become the most common – the challenge is to meet the demand for communication in a way that matches the prevailing culture and values.

Added together, these changes place demands for information that are unprecedented: information about customers and markets; about international legislation; about technology and its applications. The demand for this information is met with an array of supply techniques. Few of these are simple or straightforward, not least of which the process and methods by which organisations communicate.

The whole nature of the employment relationship is one such example. Corporate governance and the relationship with the outside world is another. How HR professionals communicate internally has been affected by change.

CONCLUSION

This chapter has analysed some of the internal and external forces at work in organisations, taxing the knowledge and skill of the HR profession. The profession has responded admirably, shaping its 'products and services' to fit the new demands for alignment with strategy whilst preserving the needs of the individual; using technologies to their fullest effect; and recognising that communication within the organisation is something that can no longer be seen as 'not part of HR'.

What the above narrative has shown is that there are many forces, both internal and external, that will affect the communication strategy of the modern organisation. It is important that those in HR keep such forces on their radar. They may determine how, when and where communication takes place.

This provides the context in which communication takes place. However, it is also necessary to understand what the key principles of organisational communication are, so that when those forces do have an impact, the HR professional will be in a position to respond with professional understanding and insight. So, what are the principles for organisational communication, and how can they be adapted to the new context of the HR professional as communicator? Chapter 4 investigates these questions.

Part 2

The principles and uses of communication

4

Principles of communication

Harry: You were going to be a gymnast.
Sally: A journalist.
Harry: Right – that's what I said. When Harry Met Sally (1989)

It is axiomatic to suggest that real changes are taking place in the everyday life of the workplace. Organisations and their employees must confront the new reality of tighter staffing, increased workloads, longer hours and a greater emphasis on performance, risk-taking and flexibility. For some, these developments present new opportunities; for others, the new corporate agenda represents uncertainty of a magnitude likely to induce disorientation in a struggle to cope with the scope and pace of change. Employee communications has a crucial role to play in the management effort to reorient employees perplexed by change, or inform and motivate those who adapt more readily.

Within this general need to communicate there exists the specialised requirement for effective communication as a sine qua non *of managing an organisation's employee relations. The world of employee relations is also the subject of significant change currently, not only mirroring the agenda of the new corporate reality but also influencing its application and reflecting a wider social and legal context in which change takes place.*

At an individual level the need for new HR policies and practices on anything from harassment to childcare requires considered and specific information to be developed, delivered and reinforced. Collectively developments such as company–union 'partnership' agreements and legislation such as the Information and Consultation Directive are imposing new demands on the organisation to inform, educate, consult and persuade. Without an understanding of what is needed to successfully communicate with their workforce and its representatives, organisations will fail to adapt to the increasing regulation of the workplace, manage change or persuade their employees that they have a viable and worthwhile future regardless of the complexity of the present.

The stakes are therefore high and it is imperative that the techniques and disciplines of effective communication are mastered in relating to employee representatives, as well as the workforce as a whole. The same issues of perceptions, listening, planning and presentation exist whether persuading a union official or informing an employee. Whether your employee relations environment is adversarial, co-operative or partnership-based does not affect this simple truth: all that changes are your objectives in communicating. Organisations who ignore this reality do so at their peril, because without high-quality communication they will never persuade employee representatives or take their workforce with them on the demanding and often uncertain journey that exists in the world of business today. Alf Worsfold BA (Hons), LLM, MBA, Pat Holroyd BSc (Hons), ACII Directors – Employment Relations Matters Ltd

INTRODUCTION

This chapter concentrates on some of the principles by which communication can take place effectively. However, this is not a textbook on communication theory, rather a practitioner's guide. There is an important reason for dealing with the basics – because our understanding of communication 'influences how we act and how we analyse situations. So it is important to work out what communication involves' (Hartley and Bruckmann 2002). One thing is certain: communication is such a fundamental part of our existence that it permeates every aspect of our lives.

So how can we get a better understanding of some of these basic principles? One way is to analyse in some detail the following:

- definitions of communication
- the building blocks of communication and how they affect the individual
- the context within which communication takes place.

This should give us a good steer for when we come to apply them in an organisational context. It sounds pretty straightforward, but it's not. Communication has many different perspectives. It is not just about transmitting simple messages from A to B. When we communicate we invariably transmit something of ourselves. 'We say or do something which affects our listener or observer. A kind of cultural ripple is created' which reflects our values (Perkins 1999).

The following definitions show how a simple concept is actually quite complex in its application.

DEFINITIONS OF COMMUNICATION

There is no single definition of communication. Instead, opinions vary:

- One view is that the definition of communication is based on 'a model first popularised in the 1950s: the so-called mathematical theory of communication. This was developed from work on telecommunications systems. It aimed to show how information is transmitted from source to destination and to analyse what can affect the quality of the information during the process' (Hartley and Bruckmann 2002).

- Or, if you prefer a slightly less formal version, communication is the process by which 'meanings are exchanged between people through the use of a common set of symbols' (Adair 1997).

- But it's also worth noting that 70 per cent of all communication in an organisation is 'at the unformalised level below or beyond the structured communication channels or mechanisms' (de Mare 1979). There is more to communication than meets the eye!

At its heart, communication is a process for passing information between two or more individuals. Communication consists of both intention and means. It is the ability of one person to make contact with another and to make him- or herself understood. This would seem to be a good working definition of communication.

These views give us the background to form an initial definition. But this is only a start. They won't be enough without more detail. Is it possible, then, to start putting some boundaries around the subject, so that when we in HR have to deal with it, we have some manageable proportions?

THE BUILDING BLOCKS OF COMMUNICATION

Let's look at some of the key ingredients that go to make up communication. Table 4 outlines some of the basic building blocks. In the first instance there has to be some form of social contact – not necessarily a physical presence, although some would argue that this is the best and most powerful form of communication. To quote Bernstein (1984), all channels of communication 'should attempt to achieve the condition of face to face'; this is of course not always possible in an organisational context. Second, there must be a common means of communicating. You are naturally aware that some breakdowns in communication occur when one party speaks a different language from the other. It's pretty obvious, really. Or so you'd think. But it can make a difference. Third, there has to be clarity within the message.

History is full of incidents where a lack of clarity in a message had great consequences. Take the Battle of Balaclava in 1854 and the Charge of the Light Brigade (you know – 'Theirs not to reason why,/Theirs but to do and die'). Lord Raglan sent orders to Lord Lucan, the divisional commander, to prevent the Russians from carrying off some captured guns. The orders were not clear and Lucan mistakenly ordered Lord Cardigan, commanding the Light Brigade, to attack well-defended Russian guns at the end of a long valley; disaster followed. Of course, communication can also be difficult if the leader happens to be insane: the commander of the Prussians at Waterloo, Field Marshal von Blücher, was convinced that he had been impregnated with a baby elephant by a French soldier (Skellon 1999).

Table 4 | *Key ingredients in communication*

Key element	Notes
Social contact	The persons who are communicating have to be in touch with each other
Common medium	Both parties to communication must share a common language or means of communication
Transmission	The message has to be imparted clearly
Understanding	The message has to be received, properly understood and interpreted

Source: Adair 1997

So here is a basic lesson in communication: make the message clear. It's no use sitting back smugly thinking, 'I sent the message and I understood it.' If the party to be communicated with doesn't hear or understand the message then it has all been a waste of time. Most people will of course see these points as basic common sense. However, effective communication means being able to repeat the success time after time. When it comes to organisational communication, this is a critical success factor. So these basic ingredients and their application in practice are the first important stages.

REALITY BITES – COMMUNICATION IN PRACTICE

How does this all get translated into reality? We can look at this by analysing what goes on when one person decides to communicate with another. So, an individual has some information that he or she wants to pass on and gain acknowledgement of. The simple process is that the message is transmitted from a sender to a receiver. Figure 8 demonstrates this basic format. In this, the building blocks outlined above are all in place. There is contact, a common means of communication, a clear transmission of the message and an understanding of it. Would that life were as straightforward as this! We know, of course, that it isn't and that things get in the way of this simple pathway of information. Several things can happen that somehow change or distort the message:

- A message between two people can be interpreted differently depending on the objective of the sender and the perception of the receiver.

- The type of channel used for communication can have an impact on the message. We know of the recent debate about e-mail versus telephony and the issues that arise in even simple communication because of the new medium. We also know of the huge growth in text messaging and the development almost of a new language because of it. The decoding of the message can be greatly affected by the channel of communication.

- There is noise that can interfere with the message being transmitted and received. 'Noise' can be personal feelings and agendas in an individual context or politics and change management in an organisational one.

*Figure 8 | **Simple communication***

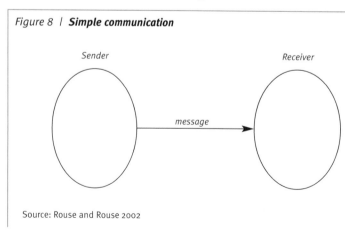

Source: Rouse and Rouse 2002

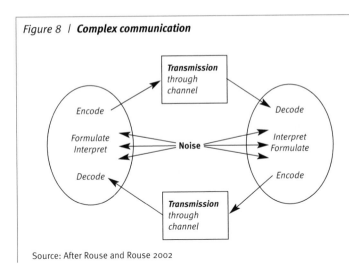

Figure 8 | ***Complex communication***

Source: After Rouse and Rouse 2002

Figure 8 shows how simple communication can be distorted. In a more complex scenario we know that messages have to be encoded by a sender and decoded by a receiver. The message is then interpreted. Well, what would happen if there was noise? An example would be quite literally a poor environment where a spoken message is not heard properly and its original meaning misinterpreted. There are children's games that actually use this when a message is whispered from one person to the next. By the time the message reaches the end of the line it is invariably different from the original. This is 'channel noise'. In fact there can be several types of noise that can get in the way of the message, including channel noise, psychological noise and language noise (Bernstein 1984). Psychological noise occurs most often when the recipient does not really want to hear the message being transmitted. In basic communication between two people there can be noise. When we come to see this applied to an organisational context the noise just gets louder and louder, making effective communication more difficult.

What we have here is a model for communication that starts simple, ie it is the basic transmission between two people, gets more complicated because of the particular view of the recipient and gets affected by the environment in which the communication takes place. This is an important consideration for anyone taking on the communication role, particularly in an organisational context (as we shall see in the next chapter). The communication is rarely simple, even though the objective might be to make it so. Recognition of the extraneous factors that can distort and confuse the message is a key first part of the role of the professional communicator. Putting in place mitigating actions that will minimise these distortions is then more achievable.

PUTTING COMMUNICATION IN CONTEXT

We now have some basic definitions of communication. But how does it actually work? First, we know that communication has to be delivered 'physically'. Things have to happen to get the message over. These are known as the *codes of communication*. Second, communication takes place in a setting or *context*. Third, communication takes place at *different levels*. Finally, communication has to be transmitted via particular *channels*. Taken together, these form the basis on which effective communication will take place.

Codes of communication

These are the ways in which we communicate in a physical sense. To use Boisot's words, 'Effective communication requires that we choose the right code. In an auction room, a wink shrewdly conveyed will secure a Cézanne; in a court of law, aimed at the judge, it will add six months to a prison sentence' (Boisot 1994).

There are many possible definitions of codes. One classification has been put forward as (Hartley and Bruckmann 2002):

- verbal
- prosodic – all the stress and pitch patterns such as pauses and intonation which we use in speech
- paralinguistic – all the pauses, um's, ah's and other sounds
- kinetic – all the ways we move our bodies in communication
- standing features – such as appearance, orientation or distance.

Of course, physical communication is only part of the story. In an organisational sense we are as likely to communicate by writing as by any other means, especially in this age of e-mail and

Table 5 | Differences between spoken and written language

Writing is	Speech is
Objective	Interpersonal
A monologue	A dialogue
Durable	Ephemeral
Scannable	Only linearly accessible
Planned	Spontaneous
Highly structured	Loosely structured
Syntactically complex	Syntactically simple
Concerned with the past and future	Concerned with the present
Formal	Informal
Expository	Normative
Argument-oriented	Event-oriented
Decontextualised	Contextualised
Abstract	Concrete

Source: Baron 1999

texting. There are differences between the two ways – see Table 5. This shows the basic features of speech and writing as forms of communication. It is absolutely vital to incorporate the messages from this chart into HR communication plans.

This table gives an understanding of the consequences of choosing a particular medium for communication. For example, using a presentation alone to explain a complex new pension or flexible benefits system in an organisational context would not be an ideal method of communication. In the opposite way, telling someone via e-mail that they had lost their job would hardly be considered good HR practice (although we have seen recent examples where some have defended such a process – in one case it was reported that redundancy notices by e-mail were requested by the employees themselves). The point is that careful consideration should be given to the medium through which communication is distributed. It has to be fit for the purpose, bearing in mind that this is open to interpretation.

Codes of communication are obviously very important in the context of two individuals. However, they reach greater importance when applied to the organisation. Written communication has been the mainstay of much of the HR communication approach: the staff notice, the letter of appointment or redundancy and so on. The real challenge is to get a good balance between the written and the oral, between a great HR website and world-class cascade communication through line managers. This is particularly important if we believe that 'without feedback there is no communication' (Bernstein 1984).

Context

Communication takes place in a contextual setting. In this respect, 'context' means the surroundings in which the communication exists. This is a critical point, especially in organisations, because it is possible that some organisational contexts lend themselves more readily to one style or type of business communication than another (this was the conclusion of a recent study – see Kramer 2001). So communication rarely takes place in a vacuum. The surroundings and the time at which it occurs affect the sending and receipt of the communication. The context may be dramatic: when Cassius Clay (later Muhammad Ali), the greatest boxer in history, met the Beatles, their joking in front of the world's press was seen to make them 'parallel players in the great social and generational shift in American society' (Remnick 1999). What kind of communication messages were these representatives of a changing era sending out? But the context can also be less dramatic, which for most of us is the norm. Examples might be as follows:

- A briefing has to take place about a particular new process being introduced into a manufacturing operation. Communication between the team leader and the employees in a particular working cell takes place in a noisy manufacturing environment. The context for this will probably determine what is heard and the interpretation of it.

- The CEO's Annual Review of Employment is transmitted via the Web. Individuals read it at home or in the office. Will the same interpretation be put on it in the absence of a dialogue? The context in which the communication is received may lead to different interpretations.

- A sales conference at the NEC, Birmingham, to celebrate past achievements and launch new targets is attended by 3,000 salespeople. The sales director and the senior management team are hosted by a TV personality who interviews them against a background of razzamatazz. The objective is motivation and the retention of information.

These three are very different examples of the kind of communication that happens, and the different contexts within which the communication take place. It goes without saying that the context of the communication can be critical to its success. Therefore those preparing the communication should make sure that this context is a live issue. It is not just about the actual message, but where and how it is given.

Levels

Whilst such simplicity provides a foundation for understanding the principles of communication, it will not be sufficient for us to develop communication strategies within the HR function. So something more comprehensive is necessary. Figure 9 shows several outcomes from the different types of communication that can exist within the organisation:

1. At the lowest level one can simply instruct another person to do something. This is not always bad. Health and safety bulletins or instructions, for example, will need to be clear and unambiguous.

2. Then there is the need to inform. This is normally to pass on information – perhaps about the workings of a new bonus scheme at one end of the scale to announcements of the company's annual results at the other.

3. The third level of communications in this model is that of consulting, where listening is much in evidence but not commitment to action. Employee representation about a

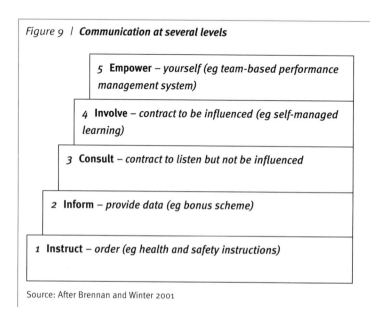

Figure 9 | *Communication at several levels*

5 **Empower** – *yourself (eg team-based performance management system)*

4 **Involve** – *contract to be influenced (eg self-managed learning)*

3 **Consult** – *contract to listen but not be influenced*

2 **Inform** – *provide data (eg bonus scheme)*

1 **Instruct** – *order (eg health and safety instructions)*

Source: After Brennan and Winter 2001

particular HR policy that is in development is an example of this. Consulting lawyers before the development of a policy would be another.

4. The fourth level outlined in the model is that of involvement. This might apply to the development of a new, self-managed training programme where groups of employees are involved in the design stage to ensure that the outcome is both practical and relevant.

5. The final level of communication is that of empowerment, a term used extensively but with a variety of interpretations. In HR terms this would be a team-based performance management system or quality circles.

The five levels show how communications can be interpreted in a variety of ways. The style and media of any communication should reflect both its purpose and the audience.

Of course there are various forms of communication that can be written, oral or non-verbal. In an organisational context, particularly one of large-scale change, a mix of forms of communication is essential.

Channels

The final basic principle concerns the channel of communication used. Table 6 shows this in detail. For the purposes of this description, four types of 'channel' have been identified. We shall come back to these later when we are in the process of designing HR communication plans. The channels are:

- *Face to face*. The most commonly understood form of communication. At an individual level, face-to-face communication takes place all the time. It is the most understood of all the communication media, because most human beings will have face-to-face communication on a daily basis.

- *Telephony*. In modern society it is unlikely that anyone could get by without telephonic communication – not only as a way of staying in touch, but also as a way of accessing services through the ubiquitous call centre.

- *The Web*. Increasingly this is being used as a basic form of communication. From e-mail to website, the number of transactions using the Web is astounding. Of course, there are great advantages to Web-based communication. Its immediacy is a strong argument in favour of using this medium. It 'can give people direct access to anyone, including senior management' and is a 'cost-effective way of linking people worldwide' (Scholes 1999). There are dos and dont's that should be taken into account when using e-mail as a form of communication – see Table 7. There are other considerations when using the Web as a communication tool. First, there is the evaluation of technology-based methods versus face to face. Table 8 outlines some of these. Then, having made the decision, there is the issue of how best we should implement a technology solution. The 'five top tips for intranet management' listed some of these as:

Table 6 | Combining segments and the media

Segment	Medium 1 Face to face	Medium 2 Telephony	Medium 3 Web	Medium 4 Mail

1 City	• Analyst
	  briefings
	• AGM
		• Telephone
		  interviews with
		  analysts
			• Company
			  results posted
			  on website
				• Analyst briefing
				  pack

2 Media	• Press briefings
	• Press interview
		• Telephone
		  interview
			• Website
			  accessed by
			  media
				• Press
				  briefings

3 Labour market
– employer brand
	• Job interview	• Recruitment
		  messages
		• Telephone
		  interview
			• Recruitment
			  website
				• Recruitment
				  materials

4 Employees	• Cascade
	  communication
	• Line manager
	  briefings
	• Staff meetings
	• Conferences
		• Line manager
		  briefings
		• HR call centre
		• Employee
		  helpline
			• HR website
			• Company
			  website
				• Individual
				  employee
				  notification
				• Staff notice

5 Board	• Presentation at
	  board
		• Meetings with
		  board members
			• Communication
			  of business
			  strategy
			• Communication
			  of board
			  membership
			• CEO's home
			  page
				• Annual People
				  Report

6 HR	• HR cross-
	  functional team
	  meetings
		• Tele-
		  conferencing
		• HR call centre
			• Intra-
			  departmental
			  e-mail
				• Memos and
				  policy
				  statements

- having a clear strategy and using it as a touchstone for success

- organising the site efficiently and effectively

- marketing the site

- having strong supportive partners

- meeting audience expectations.

TheSource@Melcrum.com 2002

Table 7 | Dos and dont's of using e-mail

Do:
 	
• *think of your e-mail message as a personal, virtual memo*
• *use a conversational and informal tone – but remain professional*
• *feel free to use contractions like 'I'm', 'we'll' and 'you've'*
• *write in complete sentences – 'Here's the information you asked for' is more respectful (and grammatically sound) than 'Information follows'*
• *be concise but courteous.*
 	
Don't:
• *let the medium's speed rush you into a response so that you:*
   – *send out a message littered with spelling mistakes*
   – *respond spontaneously and rashly, especially in anger*
• *write as you would in a conventional letter, so avoid:*
   – *beginning your e-mail with 'Dear sir' or 'Dear Mrs X'*
   – *continuing with 'I'm writing to let you know'*
   – *signing off with 'Yours faithfully' or 'Yours sincerely'*
• *use computing abbreviations, such as 'iow' for 'in other words' and 'otoh' for 'on the other hand'*
• *let your spoken style descend into slang or computer jargon*
• *use unnecessary capitals.*

Source: Morris 2000

Table 8 | E-mail versus face-to-face – the 'e' trade-off table

'E'-effective	Face/voice-effective
• *Transferring documents*	• *Co-designing*
• *Transferring procedural information*	• *Introducing new processes*
• *Congratulating*	• *Resolving different viewpoints/conflict*
• *Establishing headline opinions about specific questions*	*resolution*
	• *Congratulating or telling off*
• *Data-passing*	• *Finding out how staff are feeling and why*
• *Telling people about actions taken by others that have no direct impact*	• *Interpreting data*
	• *Gaining commitment to action*
• *Setting up meeting dates with someone you know*	• *Explaining models*
	• *Getting a meeting with someone you don't know*
• *Exploring a new subject*	• *Getting hints on how to explore a new subject*
• *Tapping into a virtual panel with defined questions*	• *Exploring broader issues*
	• *Telling someone their job will change/disappear*
• *Announcing a new appointment*	• *Suggesting something controversial*
• *Publishing something with no emotional impact*	

Source: Hedron Consulting 2001

- *Mail.* The mail continues to be one of the foundations of communication. Millions of items of mail are distributed each day. There are some basic guidelines for the written communication that should be taken into account. Lloyds TSB, for example, publishers communication guidlines emphasising the need to use plain language and to make sure that such things as grammar and punctuation are correct.

Table 6 shows how a communication plan should take account of the particular channel for each of a series of target communication 'segments'. (Segmenting the 'market' for communication will be described later.) In the context of organisational communication, these four channels will be the main ways in which communication takes place.

The channel of communication is highly important nowadays, given the fact that there is so much choice. A good deal of consideration should be given, therefore, to considering how the communication should take place. Face to face is the only way to deal with some subjects: those matters directly affecting an individual, such as hiring, firing and pay rises. But the potential offered by the Web is a tremendous way of dispersing messages in an organisational context. There are apocryphal stories about the use of the Web. Bill Gates reportedly has 300 e-mails each day, all of which he answers personally. Our challenge is to get the right mix of channels for the communication.

A HOLISTIC APPROACH TO COMMUNICATION

Taking these various definitions and contextual considerations is it possible to build a holistic view of communication? We have seen from the examples above that simple communication can be distorted by a whole range of variables: noise, context and channel can all lead to different interpretations of a message. Notwithstanding this, it is possible to build a picture of the component parts of communication.

So, a complete model of the communication process should include (Bernstein 1984):

- thoughts and impressions
- personality – identity – image
- transmitter – encoder – decoder – receiver
- formal and informal messages
- noise
- feedback
- dynamism
- relationship of participants.

At an individual level there are some mental processes that we should take into account as well. This is particularly important for the HR professional, because the communication will be about people issues and sensitivity is likely to be high. We should first and foremost try to anticipate the context within which the communication takes place and gear our communication accordingly. I can't think of a better example of this than the face-to-face cascade briefing that has been well planned in an organisational context, ie all those in work will receive the briefing. But in most organisations there will be 'key-time' or 'part-time' workers who may not be present when the briefings have been arranged. And what about parental leavers? How are they going to receive the communication? So anticipating the context is essential. Second, the HR professional should be aware of the consequences of the choices that are made. If we decide to issue a briefing to the press about an outsourcing contract, we shouldn't be surprised if the trade unions want to make their own response. Awareness of the 'angles' of communication is a critical success factor. The final two competences are to build in processes for immediate and general reflection about the communication (Guirdham 1999).

CONCLUSION

So we can conclude about the basic principles of communication that:

- communication is a process that takes place between two or more people – it is a transaction between the parties
- for the purposes of organisational communication, we can assume that it is intentional (Miller 1995); what we can't assume is that the basic communication will always arrive in its intended form
- there is a difference between communication and effective communication – the latter is 'received as accurately in terms of content and meaning as intended by the sender' (Rouse and Rouse 2002)
- the recipient of the communication will also have a particular 'angle' that may lead to a different interpretation of the information
- communication takes place in particular types of environment, and these can influence the way that the message is received (Munter 1987)

- the information that forms part of the communication is at its most useful when it is 'accurate, timely, complete, relevant' (Rouse and Rouse 2002)
- when there is no feedback there is no communication
- finally, 'the onus in communication, whether as image or message, is on the communicator. If the receiver misunderstands it is rarely his unaided mistake' (Bernstein 1984).

In an organisational context, each of these component parts will be important. When we come to put together our HR communication plans we shall have to take account of the building blocks of communication. However, we should really delve a little deeper into how these concepts work in organisations before we look specifically at the HR application. The following chapter will attempt to do just this.

5

Communication in today's organisation

'Surely you can't be serious?'
'I am serious – and don't call me Shirley.' Airplane (1980)

INTRODUCTION

There is a link between organisational performance and effective communication. David Clutterbuck has found that high-performing organisations are more likely to (Clutterbuck 2002):

- have formal communication strategies
- measure the effectiveness of their communication programmes
- have more strategic communication managers
- do a better job of explaining change
- focus on communicating with and educating employees
- provide more upward communication channels.

So if we want our organisation to achieve high performance, we may want to do something about our communication processes. But this is quite a challenge in the modern industrial and commercial environment. To communicate effectively in the modern organisation requires an understanding of what the organisation is, does and looks like – what its dynamics are and what works! Today this is not as straightforward as it once was.

FOUCAULT'S HIERARCHY

In the traditional model of the organisation things were ordered and systematic. Michel Foucault, the French post-modernist philosopher, described organisation using an architectural metaphor:

> *All the buildings were to be arranged in a circle, opening on the inside, at the centre of which a high construction was to house the administrative functions of management, the policing functions of surveillance, the economic functions of control and checking, the religious functions of encouraging obedience and work; from here all orders would come, all activities would be recorded.* Foucault in Rainbow, 1984

This type of description presents a view of the organisation as a controlled, structured environment. For many this was the norm.

There used to be a formula for effective communication in such an organisation. It was based on a leader articulating a compelling vision of the future down the organisation – classical cascade communication. The employees of the organisation would receive this communication consistently through the hierarchy of line managers and would be persuaded to follow the organisation and its leaders. And all would be well. In the Taylorist world of hierarchy and role clarity, communication could be effective through cascade alone: start at the top, prepare succinct messages and get them down the structure. Of course, in some organisations this still applies and it can work. But organisations now rarely exist in ways that are 'hierarchised' or continuous, or with clearly defined functions. Nowadays the sheer variety of structural forms of the organisation has created a new set of 'rules'. Suddenly the cascade approach alone is no guarantee of success.

Greater competition, different types of organisational form and the advent of technological revolution have created both threats and opportunities for the cascade communication approach. In particular, the nature of organisations, the type of leadership in those organisations and the concepts of how to communicate have changed radically.

SVEN'S WAY

Then came Sven-Göran Eriksson and the 'continental way' of management and communication. In stark contrast to the tub-thumping charismatic, this was a new style that could be boiled down to:

> *empowering and coaching. Empowering is about delegating responsibility to the people who work with you, sharing decision-making with them and appreciating their initiative. Coaching is about making everyone feel part of the team, encouraging players to co-operate, keeping them informed and taking an interest in their individual performance.* Birkinshaw and Crainer 2002

Suddenly the 'United Way' communication initiative, (as shown by Scott Adams and *Dilbert!*) seemed to become 'Not the United Way': 'Management, we have a problem.' What on the surface appeared to be a straightforward issue, ie transmitting information from A to B, has become a complex process riddled with pitfalls. It's hard to disagree with the assertion that 'Internal company communication is notoriously bad. There may be many reasons. The fault lies entirely with management. If the receiver gets it wrong the blame must lie with the transmitter' (Bernstein 1984).

We may conclude that organisation is 'much more than a description of power relationships. To be meaningful it must tell us about its purpose and style, interfaces and relationships, drives and measures' (Goodridge 2002). To achieve this will require communication in the organisation that reflects both business and people strategy, is professionally managed, has effective feedback loops and is seen to be fair, honest and truthful. We now know (if we didn't before!) that amongst the 'common threads' of top-performing managers are effective communications (University of Toledo research into 2,000 top-performing managers, as reported in *HR Magazine* November 2002).

Regardless of the type of organisation encountered, there is an HR responsibility for dealing with organisation design and development and, ultimately, for communicating the purposes of this. Research has shown that:

> *in a fast-changing world, organising capabilities are a more enduring source of competitive advantage than the characteristics of any particular organisation structure . . . people management and development professionals have a central role in orchestrating and developing the new processes of organising.* Whittington and Mayer 2002

The orchestration will include effective communication.

SO WHAT ARE WE TRYING TO ACHIEVE WITH ORGANISATIONAL COMMUNICATION?

There's so much that is changing about today's organisation. Nordstrom and Ridderstrale (2002) have talked of personalisation, tribalisation, self-organisation and a whole range of reminders of how funky organisations can be! Organisational communication is intended to create some kind of understanding that is designed to 'orchestrate effort in much the same way as the nervous system arranges an organism's thoughts and behaviours'. This understanding can be about the strategy and direction of the organisation or about this year's pay award, ie a diverse range of subjects. But there is a consistent point that applies to all communication. In this respect, a communication is effective when it is received by the audience for which it is intended; interpreted in the same way by those who receive as those who send; and remembered over time and used in an appropriate way (Bernstein 1984). As we have seen, the prevailing dynamics of the organisation have made this more difficult.

On the surface the organisation presents a single entity. It has boundaries, levels, operating controls and authorities. However, the communication context will actually vary 'depending on the subcultures to which the employee belongs in the organisation, subcultures defined by such things as organisational rank and orientation, job function, educational level, length of employment, age and so on' (Kramer 2001). Therefore making the statement that 'effective communication is vital to the success of the organisation' becomes a pressing strategic challenge, one that is not for the faint-hearted. Understanding how to communicate in the contemporary organisation is a vital issue. So what is the prevailing wisdom on how this should be done, and what can we learn from the general principles outlined in the previous chapter?

A STRONG CORPORATE IDENTITY IS VITAL

At a strategic level, there is evidence to show that corporate identity can be a powerful force for underpinning communication. Van Riel (1992) has put forward some views about the relevance of corporate identity that support the professional approach to HR communication. He argues that a strong corporate identity is effective in the following ways:

- *It raises motivation among employees*, in that a strong corporate identity 'creates a "we feeling". It enables employees to identify with their company.' If we see employee engagement as a critical factor in organisational success, then the creation of this feeling through effective HR communication is clearly important.

- *It inspires confidence among the company's external target groups*. This no longer refers exclusively to customers. There are other target groups to which the organisation will look. These include the City and its investors, the media and the community. HR has an increasingly influential role to play in this external identity marketing (the employment brand, for example, is part of this process).

If we believe these two perspectives, then it follows that corporate identity is important and that HR have an obligation to become involved in the organisation's communication process, as those responsible for the people elements of this identity.

VIEWS ABOUT ORGANISATIONAL COMMUNICATION

There are, then, a great many influences, both internal and external to the organisation, that will affect the way we communicate and the media we use to communicate. There is also the important conclusion made by Philip Kotler (1986) that 'what is communicated should not be left to chance'. This applies as much to HR as it does to marketing. There is a powerful and compelling case for the HR professional to step up involvement in communication and to take on more responsibility.

Its not too extreme, then, to suggest that 'a company has a duty to communicate. A duty to its many publics and to itself, because non-communication is negative communication' (Bernstein 1984). This is most important, because organisational success depends on an:

> *intricate communication network which has grown up during the years and has proved itself*
> *indispensable. The bigger the firm, the more elaborate the system must be, and the greater*
> *the likelihood of expensive and time-wasting mistakes caused through misunderstandings.*
> Little 1981

But such underlying essentials conceal many different views about how communication should be transmitted:

- One view suggests that communication should somehow be a systematic, but multi-faceted, activity: 'a 'framework of well-planned and -implemented communication programmes, using a variety of media, to meet employees' basic information needs and to facilitate the upward flow of information and ideas' (Bevan and Bailey 1991).

- But there is also the view that 'extensive top-down communication and use of multiple channels of communication are likely to increase organisational identification, with positive consequences for self-esteem, organisational commitment and co-operative behaviour. By implication, the process of communicating the psychological contract can be as important as its content' (Guest and Conway 2002).

We may say these embrace both 'continental' and Anglo-American approaches. They need not be mutually exclusive but either, or a combination of both, needs to be well managed. In communication we are dealing with a very powerful force for change. If it is effective, then the chances of achieving the strategy of the organisation can be enhanced. The reverse is true for poorly delivered communication. We saw in the previous chapter that simple communication, even between two people, can be distorted by internal or external noise. Imagine then the possibility for distortion in the complex and dynamic organisation! So there are some conclusions before we go into the mechanics of communication:

- Organisational communication is no longer something that can be left to chance. It is vital for the organisation's success that communication is successful. So much depends on it.

- HR has a growing responsibility for organisational communication. In this respect the HR professional is a guardian of the image of the organisation as perceived by employees and other 'people' stakeholders. This is to be taken as read.

- The view that the product advertising team were alone the 'image-makers' (Bernstein 1984) is no longer entirely sustainable, because HR now have to ensure that the product brand can also be adapted to reflect the 'employment brand'. HR people are now image-makers as well as image-keepers – an important development.

Here we have a significant development in the role of HR as organisational communicators. How may this be applied in practice? Are there any principles that could be taken into account when considering an HR communication strategy and plan?

FORMS OF COMMUNICATION USED IN ORGANISATIONS

It is possible to synthesise three types of communication prevalent in the contemporary organisation (van Riel 1992). Of these, probably the most important is *management communication*, which has been defined as 'communication by managers with internal and external target groups'. Two other forms of communication have been identified as *organisational communication* and *marketing communication*. The following looks at how van Riel's analysis can be used to structure HR's involvement.

Management communication

Management communication is about the need to generate a shared vision and values. We saw earlier how the characteristics of the modern organisation made this aspect of management communication particularly challenging. But the other key reason that managers want to communicate effectively is sheer motivation: a fully informed workforce is more likely to be aligned with the organisation's objectives.

Van Riel has highlighted four key elements of management communication: *consistency*, *compassion*, *selectivity* and *organisation*. The characteristics of each, for the most senior manager, the CEO, are shown in Table 9 (van Riel 1992).

This table shows that four principles should be adopted in CEO communication. HR has to support these as follows:

- *Consistency*: provide good people information and human capital measures that demonstrate alignment with the organisation's objectives and that are consistent with other communications, eg 'We are committed to customer service' might be backed up with details of the customer service training provided to employees.

Table 9 | **Van Riel's principles of CEO internal communications strategy**

Consistency	Compassion
• *Are CEO messages aligned with organisational and public relations objectives?* • *Is CEO behaviour aligned with those messages?* • *Are CEO internal and external communication roles compatible and integrated?*	• *Does CEO understand employees' communication and emotional needs?* • *Does CEO demonstrate his/her personal concern for employees' needs?* • *Do employees have accessible feedback channels to CEO?*
Selectivity	**Organisation**
• *Is CEO internal communication role distinct from other managers' roles?* • *Is CEO communication judiciously timed and regulated?* • *Does CEO take lead communication on high-impact organisational issues?*	• *Is CEO communication integrated with overall public relations plan?* • *Are CEO messages synchronised with other managers' messages?* • *Are CEO messages distributed via appropriate media?*

Actually, consistency of message is a real challenge for HR. Even on metrics such as headcount and reward there can be confusion and interpretation. Let me give you an example. When presenting the organisation's headcount figures – say to the City for the annual report – the best that can be hoped for is a snapshot of a point in time. This is like photographing a moving car, in that as soon as the shot is taken things have changed. It is up to HR to ensure that a headcount figure is presented that can be accepted by everyone (communicating to line managers that this is the figure at a fixed point in time – even though it has probably changed – is a particular challenge).

- *Compassion*: provide attitudinal briefings and craft CEO communication on values and beliefs. HR feedback loops (eg the HR website) could be used as a channel of communication to the CEO on people issues. In contrast to the metrics communication, which is in theory more straightforward, the 'softer' part of communication is actually the hardest of all. This is where HR should come into its own, and it is up to the HR professional to provide the CEO with people messages that don't forget the compassionate element. After all, organisational decisions affect lives, not just tangible assets. The HR professional has a duty to ensure that the CEO has communication that is balanced between hard issues and soft interpretation.

- *Selectivity*: ensure that the CEO has *prioritised* people issues for communication purposes. Once again we go back to the nature of communication in this age of sound-bite and headline. Complex, rambling arguments in justification of a decision, good or bad, just won't wash. The HR professional acts as a pulse check to the CEO for those issues that are the most important to the stakeholders, particularly the employees. Messages should be selected that are of importance to all parties rather than to the employer alone. The HR professional has a unique role to play in this type of communication, but it will require bravery as well as craft. It will require those in HR to put their hands up and say, 'I don't agree with this communication because it doesn't really answer what the employees want to hear.'

- *Organisation*: ensure that the CEO's people communication is integrated with the overall people communication strategy (or vice versa!). This is critical, and again the HR professional has a key role to play. This is about joining up the people messages with the business messages and making sure that they are put forward in the right organisational context. A real example that I came across here was when pay negotiations began at the same time as the announcement of record profits. The early seeding about how tough it was going to be (even though it was) was not believed or accepted by employee representatives. This could have been avoided if the timing of the communication had been handled better. HR professionals can have a really valuable input in this area.

These principles have been proposed for the CEO. However, they can be adapted to any senior management communication, depending on the shape and size of the organisation involved.

Organisational communication

This has been defined as 'public relations, public affairs, investor relations, labour market communication, corporate advertising, environmental communication and internal communication' (van Riel 1992). Several of these factors are of particular interest to HR in their communications role:

Public relations

Public relations is that activity between an organisation and the 'publics' (customers, community, shareholders etc) with whom it has a relationship. In HR terms this is important, because any of these relationships can be enhanced or damaged by people practices. At the highest level, public relations embraces work with government, legislators, professional bodies and suchlike. The HR role will be to make sure that communication takes place with these areas to give a view of the particular circumstances of the organisation or industry. A recent development by the American Society for Human Resource Management has stretched this concept to new boundaries. In October 2002 the Society began underwriting Public Radio International's 'Marketplace Morning Report', a radio piece that would be broadcast to 287 radio stations in the USA and reach over 3 million people (*HR News* December 2002).

Community affairs is also included here. In this respect the HR role will be to make sure that the employment brand is reflected in the overall positioning of the organisation in the communities in which it operates.

But the closest many in HR will have come to public relations will have been in dealing with the public relations that comes out of the employment tribunal case that makes either the local or national press. It's likely that HR will have had to respond in a public relations context to issues about unfair dismissal, sexual harassment or equal pay. The public relations requirement of HR in terms of communication will be to ensure a balanced approach to this type of case, whatever the decision – otherwise the reputation of the employer might be damaged. So it is not something that can be left to chance. HR will need to be active in this type of communication.

Such events, where they affect the perception of an organisation as an employer, will require joint management between the external PR specialists and HR. Potential employees in the community will also be interested in the performance of an organisation and what it would be like as an employer. The employment brand is a growing area of interest in organisations as they try to get to potential employees in the war for talent.

Investor relations

In the summer of 2002 we saw just how jittery investors could get about the state of corporate governance. This went way beyond the normal level of performance evaluation and included issues traditionally regarded as fairly 'soft' – you know, morale and morality, ethics, leadership – all people issues, as it turned out.

Later we shall look at the increasingly important role of HR when it comes to dealing with all those investor groups, from individual shareholders to merchant banks and fund managers. Once the sole province of the finance department, investor relations now contains an increasing amount of people issues, including executive pay, top management recruitment, training and so on. It is important that those in HR become engaged in the process of investor relations either as advisers to executive directors or in dealing directly with investor questions. The City will want to know about the performance of the company, any changes in the way it is run, any particular events or incidents that might affect corporate performance. Increasingly, brand values (financial) are of interest to investors as well as the traditional financial measures of organisational performance. A recent survey by Interbrand gave the following brand values:

Company	Brand value £(bn)	Market value £(bn)
Barclays	5.99	28.7
RBS	5.69	44.7
Vodaphone	5.46	63.7
LTSB	4.59	32.8

Source: The *Times 29 July 2002*

The article concluded that 'many of these companies are service-focused, so they will have to work hard on their brand delivery through their employees'. It's likely that HR will have an input into this kind of measure in the organisation's relationship with its investors.

Likewise, the media are hungry for stories. They will be watching the organisation for anything that may prove to be interesting to their readership. As well as the trade press or professional journals, both the tabloids and broadsheets should be seen as potential recipients of corporate communications. HR has an increasing role in providing information and interpretation to this segment.

Labour market communication

We know that the war for talent is no longer just a theoretical concept. Therefore, maintaining a good image in the labour marketplace is vital for a healthy flow of incoming employees and the retention of existing employees. These potential employees will no longer join the organisation as an act of faith. They will want evidence of good employment practice and opportunity, and the HR professionals in the organisation will have to develop ways of communicating this. Later we shall discuss the growing use of the employment brand as a way of engaging potential employees and the community into the values and beliefs of the organisation as an employer.

Internal communication

Internal communication is a fundamental part of organisational communication that will demand the active involvement of HR. As we shall see later, the staff notice is no longer evidence that HR people are fulfilling this role. Within the organisation we have a generation of employees raised on a rich diet of communication in every aspect of their lives. They will expect the organisation to keep them up to speed on what is going on and will, increasingly, demand a voice in the future direction of the organisation.

In HR we use a wide variety of communication:

- external job advertising incorporating the employment brand
- induction packs for new starters
- job descriptions or role specifications
- policy and procedures manuals or intranet websites
- pay and reward briefings
- performance management review documentation
- training activities and materials
- staff notices and bulletin boards – physical or virtual
- annual people reports
- benefits statements.

Each of these contains a communication message. Sometimes they contain conflicting messages: corporate success and job reductions; recruitment and redundancy simultaneously; pay increases in some areas, reductions in others; and a wide variety of views about the organisation's position with regard to its people. Such multiple communication needs to be managed in a co-ordinated, professional, joined-up way. HR have this responsibility.

Internal communication is the lifeblood of the organisation. 'All organisations are created and organised through a communication process and are maintained by people communicating with each other' (Rouse and Rouse 2002). There are different ways that we can communicate in the organisation.

For example, *downward communication* is one of the most common forms and is likely to be the most understood. Downward communication has a number of attributes (Torrington and Hall 1991):

- It enables decisions taken by managers to result in action by employees.
- It ensures that this action is consistent and co-ordinated.
- It leads to reduced costs because fewer mistakes are made.
- It may stimulate a greater commitment from employees, and from this a better service to customers results.

From all of these greater effectiveness and profitability should stem. More and more organisations, though, have recognised the criticality of ensuring that there is a process of *upward communication* as well. This is important for the following reasons (Torrington and Hall 1991):

- It helps managers to understand employees' business and personal concerns.
- It helps managers to keep more in touch with employees' attitudes and values.
- It can alert managers to potential problems.
- It can provide managers with workable solutions to problems.
- It can provide managers with the information they need for decision-making.
- It helps employees to feel that they are participating and contributing and can encourage motivation.
- It provides some feedback on the effectiveness of downward communication and ideas on how it may be improved.

There is no doubt about the importance of communication in the contemporary organisation, and each level in the organisation has its own part to play. Senior management should be committed to the importance of communication. Those in HR have to be guardians of communication when it affects employees. How they do so can be by a variety of ways, and it is up to those in HR to understand the best way of communicating within their organisation.

A further aspect of internal communication lies at the highest level. The board of directors will expect absolutely high levels of communications. Not only executive but non-executives alike will want information across a broad range of subjects. HR issues are increasingly common items on the board agenda. Finally, within HR itself communication is increasingly seen as a critical success factor. The need to join up the various specialist strands of HR has never been greater, and therefore communicating clearly is a necessary part of the role of the HR professional.

Marketing communication

A further type of organisational communication that could be a useful guide for the HR professional is in marketing. The marketing (or nowadays 'customer relationship management') function has probably the most mature approach to communications of any of the functions of the organisation. 'Promotion' was one of the classical '4 Ps' of marketing (along with product, price and place), and communicating with customers was a critical success factor in the adoption of the organisation's products or services.

To achieve this, a mix of four factors was managed as an integrated unit. The marketing communications mix was described as (Kotler 1986):

- *Advertising* – any paid form of non-personal presentation and promotion of ideas, goods or services by an identified sponsor

- *Sales promotion* – short-term incentives to encourage purchase or sales of a product or service

- *Publicity* – non-personal stimulation of demand for a product, service or business unit by planting commercially significant news about it in a publicised medium or obtaining favourable presentation of it upon radio, television or stage that is not paid for by the sponsor

- *Personal selling* – oral presentation in a conversation with one or more prospective purchasers for the purpose of making sales.

Table 10 shows how this might be used in HR communication. It is possible to develop an HR communication mix that adapts the framework used in marketing. What this approach facilitates is a structured approach to developing a communication mix for HR in a way that mirrors that of marketing (who, after all, have much more experience in this type of approach).

Table 10 | The HR communication mix

	Marketing	**HR**
Advertising	*Product or services in newspapers, TV and radio*	*Internal – job vacancies, new HR services* *External – job vacancies, employer brand*
Promotion	*Financial or other incentives given to distributors of products or services (sales teams or agents)*	*Incentivising employees to adopt a particular HR policy – such as share plans by discounted share price*
Publicity	*Press releases about product launches or product successes*	*Benefits of employment with the organisation by newspaper articles or press releases*
Personal selling	*Sales teams directly persuade customers of benefits of buying products or services*	*Personnel or training professionals liaising directly with employees about a particular HR service, such as healthcare*

There are several steps that can be undertaken to achieve this type of model:

- Analyse the current mix of HR communication by placing examples into each of the four segments (advertising, promotion, publicity and personal selling).
- Plot an 'ideal' communication mix onto the same table. So, for example, the HR strategy might see an increase in external recruits to provide a refreshing of the workforce to tackle new markets. This would mean an increase in advertising, and hence the advertising part of the table would have this objective or plan included.
- Compare how the future 'ideal' matches the current level of activity.
- Adjust the HR communication mix accordingly.

In segmenting the mix, there will be a greater chance to ensure co-ordination between the various activities. For example, a recruitment campaign could have all elements of the mix, including:

- *advertising* – job advertisements in newspapers or on the Web for e-recruitment
- *promotion* – 'invite a friend' to join the organisation would be such a promotion in HR terms
- *publicity* – local PR about the organisation as an employer
- *personal selling* – employee roadshows.

By looking at the organisation's mix in this way, all angles will be covered.
The connection with the brand of the organisation will also be established. Figure 10 shows the connection between communication and brand competence.

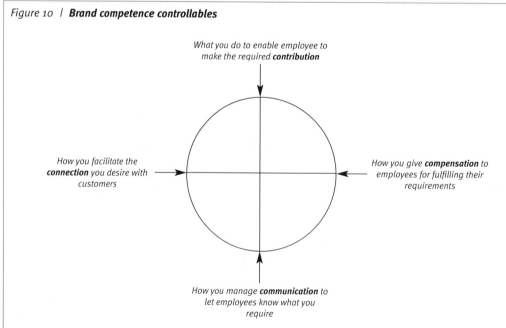

Figure 10 / **Brand competence controllables**

What you do to enable employee to make the required **contribution**

How you facilitate the **connection** *you desire with customers*

How you give **compensation** *to employees for fulfilling their requirements*

How you manage **communication** *to let employees know what you require*

Source: Betts 1999

AN ORGANISATIONAL MODEL FOR COMMUNICATION

We have a vast amount of information about organisational communication. We have seen the forces that are at work, the types of communication and the nature of effective communication. How might we use this in our HR role as guardian and image-maker? Figure 11 shows how a sequence for putting in organisational communication might occur.

The important principles here are to:

- understand and agree the message to be communicated

- make sure that there are clear objectives for the communication

- segment the proposed 'audiences' so that the communication hits the right spot

- decide who should send the message – is it the CEO, senior manager or the functional manager?

- decide what medium to use

- make sure, finally, that feedback loops are built into the communication – otherwise it isn't communication at all.

These are some of the ways that communication can be applied in the organisation.

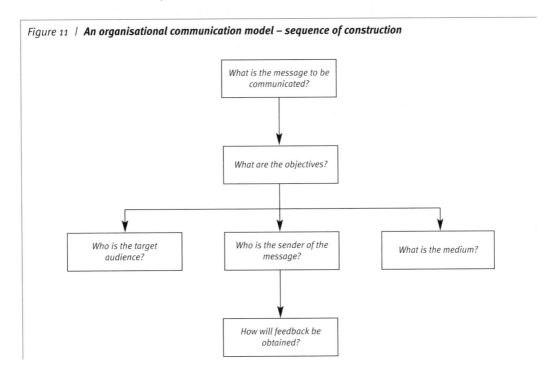

Figure 11 / **An organisational communication model – sequence of construction**

In some organisations, such as Lloyds TSB, guidelines for communication are articulated (via the corporate intranet) for all employees to see and understand. These guidelines can be in several forms but usually contain a combination of the following principles:

- Identify who the audience is, what the message is and what media are available for the communication.
- Then apply the organisation's principles of communication – have a plan, ensure communication is co-ordinated.
- Develop the communication with the right 'tone of voice'.
- Distribute the communication.
- Check its effectiveness through feedback mechanisms.

Quite straightforward, really!

CONCLUSION

This chapter has shown how the principles of communication could be applied in an organisation. However, we have not tried to reinvent the wheel and come up with a new HR model. Instead we have taken some well-tried and -tested techniques in other functions (PR, marketing) and applied them in an HR context. They work. It is as viable to have an HR communication mix as it is to have a marketing communication mix. It is necessary to have HR elements of public relations as well as financial and so on. These things will not happen automatically, though. They will require an HR function that is both proactive and interventionist in the organisation's processes wherever there is a communication affecting people issues.

So there we have it. But what should HR do in terms of strategy and planning for this important and complex activity? Chapter 6 addresses this important question.

6

Developing a communication strategy for HR

Take me to the window. Let me look at the moors with you once more, my darling. Once more. Wuthering Heights (1939)

INTRODUCTION

In the previous chapters we looked at the increasingly important role for HR in organisational communication. The necessity to use more sophisticated ways to engage employees, HR colleagues, the board, the media and the City in the organisation's activities was emphasised. This chapter concentrates on the first priority for HR in this process – which is to develop an HR communication strategy (before leaping into tactical solutions). The reason for so doing is that, first and foremost, communication is actually a strategic issue. It is something that will either contribute to or get in the way of the organisation's success. Furthermore, as we have seen, communication is a business issue. In both respects, those in HR will need to see 'the bigger picture' first. Only then can communication plans be put in place. In order to facilitate the debate about HR's role, a proposal for developing an HR communication strategy is outlined in Figure 12. This shows an 'idealised' process with the following core components:

- the participation of HR in developing a business strategy

- the development of an aligned HR strategy

- the development of an HR communication strategy in support of the business strategy

- measurement and feedback on the success of the communication.

The actions and process contained in this figure will form the basis of the current chapter. However, as with so many other aspects of strategy, it all needs to be adapted to the organisation's unique experiences. Furthermore, it is unlikely that the process will be as sequential as implied. Instead, a parallel process is more likely. But before we go into any detail on this, it may be helpful to define what we mean by 'strategy' and specifically 'communication strategy'.

In my book *HR Forecasting and Planning,* I argued strongly that HR people need to know about strategy (Turner 2002). If they didn't, then they wouldn't be able to participate in the

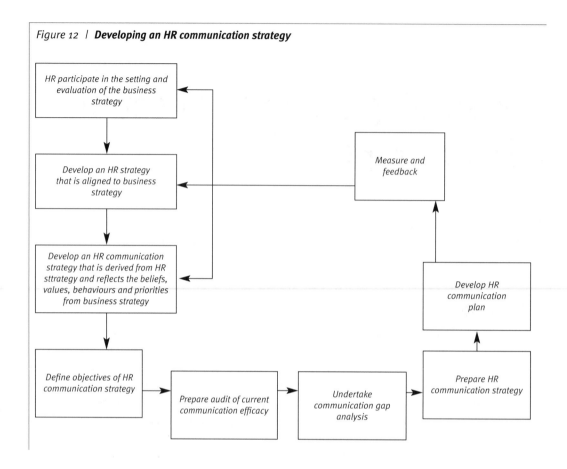

Figure 12 | *Developing an HR communication strategy*

organisation's strategy-setting process as equal partners. This would inhibit not only the HR function but also the organisation as a whole, because success would depend on 'an HR contribution that is as much about strategy as it is about tactics' (Turner 2002). Furthermore, 'HR strategy should be an integral part of the business strategy, contributing to the business planning process as it happens' (Armstrong and Baron 2002). This principle applies also to the development of communication. There should be a communication strategy for HR, therefore, that is aligned with the business strategy; that has measurable objectives and that takes account of the needs of the recipients as much as the organisation.

WHAT IS STRATEGY?

Michael Porter's work on competitive strategy and competitive advantage set the strategic agenda during the 1980s and 1990s, and he has continued to develop these themes. Those who attended the 2000 CIPD conference at Harrogate will have seen Porter develop strategy with more of a people focus. He has defined the strategy-setting process as 'the search for a favourable competitive position in an industry ... competitive strategy aims to establish a profitable and sustainable position against the forces that determine industry competition' (Porter 1985). It is 'a broad formula for how a business is going to compete, what its goals should be, and what policies will be needed to carry out those goals'. Porter has outlined six principles on which the fundamentals of strategy could be achieved (Porter 2001):

- Start with the right goal.
- A company's strategy must enable it to deliver a value proposition or set of benefits.
- Strategy needs to be reflected in a distinctive value chain.
- Robust strategies must involve 'trade-offs'.
- Strategy defines how all the elements of what a company does fit together.
- Strategy involves continuity of direction.

In Porter's terms an organisation has to take a clear strategic position, understand that position and then make sure that its activities along the value chain (sales, marketing, production, HR and so on) are aimed at achieving or enhancing the strategy.

However, given the fact that there is unlikely to be one universal strategy that is relevant to all organisations – no strategic 'theory of everything' – the Porter model is not the only one used by organisations. The work of Henry Mintzberg suggests a different approach. Mintzberg described strategic planning as an oxymoron, which makes his position clear on the subject. Instead of the rigorous 'economic' analysis that inevitably accompanies the type of strategic positioning envisaged by Porter, he believes that organisations should 'craft strategy' and adapt it to the circumstances that arise in a competitive market. In an attempt to guide those whose job it is to put strategy into practice, he described the process of a 'strategy safari' and has identified ten schools of thought in respect of strategy development. These schools have varied in popularity over time. It is argued that three 'prescriptive' schools were largely dominant during the 1970s and 1980s, other 'descriptive' schools rising to the fore in the 1990s. So we have:

- *prescriptive approaches*, which tend to be formal and analytical. This type of strategy-setting was predominant during the 1970s and 1980s and indeed is still adopted, in modified formats. These focus on market analysis and positioning; Porter's work on *Competitive Advantage* (1985) might fit into this type of approach.

- *descriptive approaches*, which involve visioning and emergent and transforming processes, and which are based on interaction within the organisation as well as external analysis. This type of model came into prominence during the 1990s. Mintzberg's work on *Crafting Strategy* typifies this type of outlook on strategy-setting (Minzberg, 1987).

Mintzberg's view would see the organisation being flexible in its approach to strategy according to the changes in the environment in which it operated.

This polarised view, prescriptive or descriptive, is of course a little simplistic. The reality is that organisations tend to select parts from both approaches. In some cases they will apply economic analysis to decide on a strategic direction; in others they will be more flexible.

DEVELOPING AN HR COMMUNICATION STRATEGY

Once organisations have been through the process of strategy-setting that best suits them then they normally move to the implementation stage. This involves the development of functional strategies, of which HR is one – communication is a key part of this. In recent times the development of an HR communication strategy and associated actions is increasingly important. HR have to be professional in the way they communicate because of the complexity of the process. There are, for instance, psychological barriers to communication, including 'people's emotions, perceptions and selectivity' (Munter 1987).

Figure 12 on page 68 outlines the proposal and the following describes some of the key aspects of each section.

HR participate in the setting and evaluation of the business strategy

Before anything, those in HR have to get into a position whereby they are able to influence business strategy. HR professionals are one of a group of functional specialists who expect to have an input into the strategy-setting process. Figure 13 shows how this might take place. HR's input will be about such external factors as the availability of the right quantity and quality of labour, and legislative considerations; and internal factors about employee relations, reward, training and so on. Once these inputs and those from other functional areas have been fed into the dialogue about strategy, the organisation can begin to develop some strategic options. The options are further refined during the strategic planning process or, in the absence of one, by a dialogue between the board and its senior managers. In developing a strategic position, either through prescriptive or descriptive approaches, organisations have to make strategic choices that determine how and where they allocate resources.

There is normally a choice of strategic options facing organisations. The factors that determine which strategy or strategies are ultimately chosen include the organisation's:

- history and past experience
- present market position
- identified market opportunity
- expectation of the amount of change to come.

There are also the personal preferences of the chief executive officer!

At some point the organisation decides on a course of strategy or, more probably, several possible approaches, and then the process of resource allocation and implementation takes place.

It is a fundamental point that HR should be involved in the strategy-setting process. After all, without the people elements of the strategy in place, it is unlikely that the strategy will succeed.

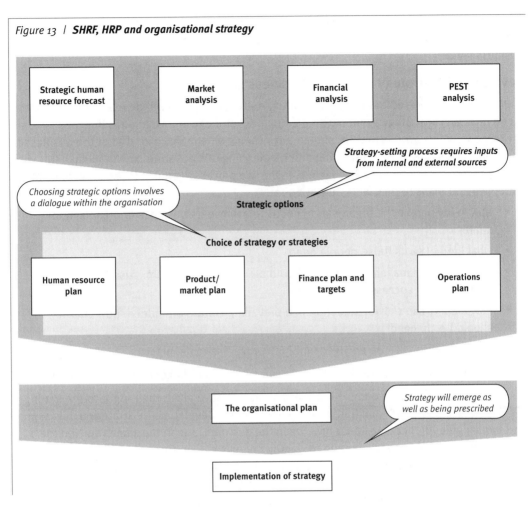

Figure 13 / **SHRF, HRP and organisational strategy**

There is growing recognition of this, as discussed in earlier chapters. However, before HR professionals can expect to participate in the strategic debate they need to be conversant with the process for the setting of strategy that is being used. In fact, if those in HR don't understand the criteria for strategic participation, it is unlikely to be able to influence the people elements at all. Once they have done so, then there are several positive steps that can be taken to ensure that HR are involved in the strategy-setting process:

- Ensure that an effective strategic HR business partner approach is in place. Senior HR professionals must be seen as having a strategic contribution to make if they are to participate fully in the strategy-setting process.
- Ensure that the importance of people engagement is seen as a critical success factor by providing evidence to support this view.
- Ensure that transactional HR is so effective that it does not provide a distraction.

These steps will go some way to dealing with the fundamentals of HR in the quest for a strategic role. Not to put too fine a point on it, if HR aren't involved in the strategy-setting role, then the chances of organisational success will be diminished, because the people elements won't get enough air time. So HR's strategic contribution is no longer an optional extra: it is mainstream business sense.

Develop an HR strategy aligned to business strategy

If HR have been involved in the overall strategy-setting process it will be easier to achieve that HR nirvana: an HR strategy aligned with the business strategy. But what does this mean in practice? One view (my own) is that HR should align their own strategy with that of the business by using effective strategic HR forecasting and HR planning. It's not surprising that I take this view, having written a book about it! In essence, these two processes enable those in HR to establish strategies and plans to deal with (Turner 2002):

- how many people the organisation needs to achieve its business or organisational strategy
- what kind of skills those people need
- what kind of management culture should prevail in the quest for sustained organisational success
- how leaders can provide direction in a prevailing culture or, indeed, how culture should be changed
- how employees can be engaged within the organisation's mission.

This then gives us a foundation on which we can support our HR communication strategy.

So let's take stock. By this point, HR professionals will have given their input to the setting of the business strategy and from this will have been able to develop an HR strategy that is aligned and meaningful. An HR plan should have been the outcome, and in the same way that the business strategy allows the organisation to deploy its resources in the most appropriate manner, then the HR strategy will do likewise. There will be some key themes for HR, a prioritised set of HR projects to meet the needs of the strategy and a well-thought-through task and activity list. The challenge we face now, of course, is that the strategy has been confined to a few individuals: the HR community probably know what's going on, as the board certainly will, but that's about it. We now need to get this knowledge to a wider community.

Develop an HR communication strategy derived from HR strategy

The way to do this is to make sure that the points of the strategy as they affect the people within and outside the organisation are communicated effectively. This requires as much input as any other part of the HR strategy and demands a level of professionalism on a par with any other HR function (reward, ER and so on). In this context, what is the definition of a communication strategy, and what are its constituent parts? For this, we can adapt the generic business view of strategy for the purposes of HR communication strategy.

Definition of the HR communication strategy

A definition of corporate communication has been put forward as 'the integrated approach to all communication produced by an organisation, directed at all relevant target groups. Each item of communication must convey and emphasise corporate identity' (van Riel 1992). In this definition, corporate identity included 'the strategically planned and presented, applied self-presentation of the company'. However, this only goes so far in the quest for a definition of an HR approach to corporate communication. So a refined version might run:

the positioning and deployment of the organisation's beliefs, attitudes and values in a structured and systematic way against the organisation's agreed business strategy to both internal and external publics or audiences.

This definition embraces a number of different concepts. The first point is that the HR communication strategy deals with softer issues of beliefs and values as well as the harder things about pay, training and so on. Second, it positions the human elements of the communication against the business strategy. The objective here is to portray the HR communication strategy as a business-based entity, not just another fad from HR. That way it will have a greater chance of being integrated into mainstream business activity. Third, it is done in a systematic way. This doesn't mean robotic. It means thought through and joined up. And finally, it includes both internal and external publics. As we shall see in later chapters, the HR communication strategy is as much about communicating with potential employees, the media and the City as any other 'public'. It is a broad statement of intent and action.

The ways in which HR communication interacts with the overall strategic process was described in earlier chapters. This model was based on the CIPD's view of the link between HRM and performance.

Define the objectives of the HR communication strategy

Objectives are what we want to achieve by implementing the HR communication strategy. They give a series of targets by which the success of the strategy can be assessed. If these are measurable, then you're more likely to know how you're doing and have pointers to how you may want to adapt the strategy. So communication objectives determine *what* is to be achieved by the communication – not *how*.

Typically, communication objectives in an HR context may be to:

- communicate the values and beliefs of the organisation in a way that is understood by the stakeholders of the organisation
- articulate the behaviours required of all employees of the organisation that are consistent with the values and beliefs
- engage employees in the people aspects of the business strategy
- ensure that all the managers in the organisation understand the link between staff satisfaction and customer satisfaction
- engage the board with the people aspects of the business strategy
- communicate the investment in human capital to the City
- communicate the people aspects of business strategy to the media.

Agreeing a set of objectives for the HR communication strategy is an essential prerequisite. They will determine the nature of the communication, the channels by which the communication are delivered and the measures of success that are agreed.

Prepare an audit of current communication efficacy

The question that then arises is: where are we now? This can be filtered down to two key areas. The first is an audit of stakeholder attitudes. This will give an understanding of where the hot spots for communication are likely to be. Second, the channels of communication can also be audited. If we are to reach a multi-faceted, diverse and widely distributed workforce, we need to know whether the channels of communication are effective. Likewise, we need to know that our communication channels to other stakeholders are robust. So what are the types of thing we should be looking for in this audit?

Attitudinal

Where are we now, for example, in terms of employee perceptions of the values and beliefs we are planning to communicate? Such information can be gleaned from staff attitude surveys. So, for example, we may have a business objective for customer service improvement. To do this involves training in customer service management and inculcating a belief that the organisation is committed to customer service. The HR communication strategy will embrace both of these. So we shall want to know how far we have to go to achieve the objectives. An audit of current perception gives a starting point against which measures of success can be mapped.

Where are we now in terms of media and perceptions of our organisation and its people strategies? Again, this is a necessary benchmark against which our HR communication strategy can be measured. Assessing this will probably be done in a less systematic way than staff attitudes. However, in developing an HR communication strategy, it should be a conscious effort. Both numbers and type of report in the press can be useful measures. Financial comment and share price are the equivalent measures for City attitudes!

Channels of communication

It's important to know how effective we are in reaching the various audiences for the communication. This is more difficult with paper-based than Web-based channels. For paper-based communication it is necessary to know how wide the distribution of the communication is. In multi-site organisations this is going to be a challenge, so a good starter for eventual agreement of the strategy is knowing how good the process is. The Web is less of a problem. In theory, everyone with access to the Internet or company intranet (if one exists) can receive a communication.

The HR communication audit is a pulse check of employee perception of the efficacy of the communication, as well as perception of the actual data.

Undertake a communication gap analysis

We now have the objectives for the HR communication strategy and an audit of our current position. This enables any gaps to be identified in either the attitudinal or channel aspects of

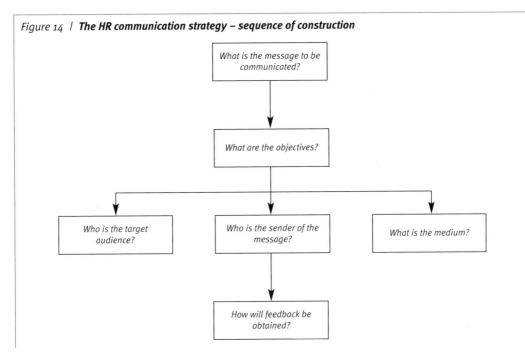

Figure 14 | ***The HR communication strategy – sequence of construction***

the communication. These gaps tell us where the resource needs to be placed. In the communication context there are two areas where 'gaps' may be identified:

- between the intended message and the received message – *attitudinal*
- between the intended audience and the audience reached – *channel*.

Gap analysis shows where the main areas of concern are.

Prepare the HR communication strategy

Having done the preparation, we can move to setting a communication strategy. But what does an HR communication strategy actually look like? A sequential approach may be helpful. This is included in Figure 14. Let's apply an example against this.

The subject is the annual pay round. The board has approved a 3 per cent increase. However, this is not going to apply across the organisation. Instead, a new process using market indicators is proposed. HR were able to influence the board on this approach, which lets good performers or those in higher cost of living areas be rewarded slightly differently. The business strategy is to keep good performers in all areas and to develop those who are high potential earners but who may be paid below market indicators at present because of short service and so who may leave for jobs with other organisations.

This has to be communicated. What would be the HR communication strategy? Using the framework in Figure 14, the following might take place:

- *What is the message to be communicated?*
  The first point here is to decide on the key message to be put over as part of the pay

communication strategy. In essence, the pay-round this time is not 'same for all' but 'pay for performance'. This is a strong message that is aligned with both the HR strategy and business strategy

- *What are the objectives?*
  The objectives of the communication are to engage all employees with a new performance-related approach to pay rather than the across-the-board standard of the past. This is a difficult message to sell, because some people may be disadvantaged by so doing. However, the key message has got to be 'If your performance is good, your pay will be good.'

- *Who is the target audience?*
  The target audience is in essence all employees, because this is an organisation-wide scheme. However, as we have already seen, it is preferable to segment the audience so that a more focused communication can be delivered. So there are two other target groups: first, high performers who will receive more pay from the pay-round; and second, those employees who are operating below the market indicator. The communication to employee representatives or their trade unions has to be excellent. The imminent findings of the information and consultation legislation emanating from Brussels necessitate a good deal of attention to this area, although being forced by legislation should never replace the best practice of consultation with trade unions.

- *Who is the sender of the message?*
  The sender of the message is the chief executive. However, there is also a strong local flavour to the strategy that sees line managers managing pay in their own units. The incidence of a strong, empathetic relationship between line managers and employees is high, which can be a great strength in selling the new pay process. The message therefore has three elements: first, the CEO gives the reasons for the change, the overall position of the organisation and how this fits in with total remuneration; second, there is an element that can be presented by the individual line manager; third, there is an overall notice outlining the package in its totality. This can either be posted on the Web or included in an HR-branded document.

- *What is the medium?*
  Because the message has to spread throughout the organisation, a multimedia approach is best used. Whatever method the CEO uses to communicate – Web, newsletter, personal letter, business TV – is the prime media channel. However, the fact that line managers can play such an important role gives the opportunity for face-to-face communication as well. It will be the job of those in HR communication to ensure that the timing, content and process for the cascade are co-ordinated. Employee representatives will of course have been briefed in confidence on any of the communication proposals.

- *How will feedback be obtained?*
  Finally, there will need to be an excellent feedback loop if the communication is to be

successful. This can have several elements:

- The CEO's webpage, if one exists, can have a Q&A section on which employees can post questions or give feedback.

- The line managers' briefing will have an element of dialogue and Q&A associated with it. Line managers can then feed back any specific messages up the chain.

- There can be an open website, comments 'box' or reply form for giving comments or raising queries.

- There can be a telephonic response, such as an HR call centre or helpline.

These ensure that the process is not just top-down but can take account of any feedback from employees.

- *Develop an HR communication plan*
Once the HR communication strategy has been agreed, there is the matter of planning to ensure excellence in delivery. The next chapter talks more about how exactly an HR communication plan can be put together.

EXAMPLES OF HR COMMUNICATION STRATEGY

What would an aligned HR communication strategy actually look like in its joined-up form? Here are some examples:

- The organisation is struggling to fill its vacancies and retain staff because of skills shortages. To deal with this it decides to increase pay to the upper quartile, introduce a training bonus for all staff, provide family-friendly policies on working time and offer retail vouchers and store discounts. These are a variety of HR actions that need to be communicated 'holistically'. This entails a communication strategy:

  - Decide on a position for the communication – in essence 'We are a leading employer.'

  - Make sure that whatever communication is issued has this theme in its tone of voice and content.

  - Make sure that the communications on each individual area (pay, training, etc) are co-ordinated. This is particularly true for trade union or employee representatives. It is essential to include the representatives in the communication process.

  - Make sure that there is a common format. There's nothing worse than seeing HR communication in different formats on different subjects (but with common links) being issued in a way that looks amateurish.

  - Make sure that there is a feedback mechanism – either a Q&A format on the Web, through briefings or by phone.

Here's another example:

- The annual results presentations to the media and City analysts aim to announce both profit increases and job cuts through productivity gains by investment in technology. The HR communication challenge here is to manage the essential dichotomy. Here's a possible strategy to deal with this:

- Make sure that all industrial relations matters have been dealt with *before* the announcements. The role and position of the trade union or employee representative is critical to the success of the communication.

- Make sure that the communication about productivity increases and job reductions is dealt with in a sensitive manner, ie it's better for staff to have their communication about such issues, especially if they are affected, through face-to-face briefings before they read about it in the Sunday press.

- Make sure that there is a co-ordinated approach to the communication. There's nothing worse than getting a company recognition letter on the same day as the announcement about the office closure.

These are just a few of the ideas for making sure that there is alignment.

CONCLUSION

Taking a strategic overview of communication from an HR perspective would seem to be an essential prerequisite to action. This is because of the need to join up a range of HR activities – reward, IR, training and so on – and communicate these in a consistent and co-ordinated way. Without a strategy for HR communication, there is a danger of fragmentation and mixed messages. So it's up to those with responsibility for HR communication to stand back and take this overview.

Having come up with a strategy we shall be in a position to develop an HR communication plan that allows us to implement effectively. The next chapter looks at the component parts of the plan.

7

Implementing an HR communication plan

There is a difference between knowing the path and walking the path. The Matrix (1999)

INTRODUCTION

The HR communication plan serves three purposes. First, it articulates the detail of the implementation programme. Second, it provides a framework for co-ordinating all the constituent parts of HR. Third, it provides role clarity both within the HR function and those parts of the organisation on which HR is dependent (ie logistics for distributing paper copies of any communication; technology for providing bandwidth to serve HR communication, and so on). The HR communication plan is the road map by which the communication strategy is achieved.

It's important that the HR communication plan takes account of all the critical elements. Table 11 shows the evolution of a communication approach for HR that is multi-faceted, including all channels, recognising the different flows of information within the organisation and providing

Table 11 | Communications in classical, human relations and human resources approaches

	Classical approach	Human relations approach	Human resources approach
Communication content	Task	Task and social	Task, social and innovation
Communication direction	Vertical (downwards)	Vertical and horizontal	All directions, team based
Communication channel	Usually written	Often face to face	All channels
Communication style	Formal	Informal	Both, but especially informal

Source: Miller 1995

for feedback. This diagram shows that the content is only one part of the communication plan. Clearly this is important, but the need to ensure the right channel for the communication, the consistency with the style and 'tone of voice' of the organisation and the means of getting the message over is of equal importance. Such an approach is essential if we are to take account of the complexities of the organisation.

Successful communication happens only when the process *and* the dynamics of the organisation are dealt with. There are vested interests in almost every aspect of the HR communication. These interests may, if not recognised, create an unco-ordinated environment and ultimately cause the failure of the communication. For example, the IR professional will want to make sure that the communication coincides with any trade union briefing that takes place and will look to influence the plan in this way. However, there may be others who would prefer to have direct communication with employees and not want it held up by a process of consultation. Getting these in synch will be a major part of the HR communication plan. Furthermore, it requires judgement on the part of HR to make sure that there is not too much, too little or inappropriate communication: three factors that can lead to failure.

The context of the HR communication plan has to be more than just tasks. It has to deal with social aspects as well. In this respect it's important that we recognise and deal with the potential blockages that may occur. We can emulate Charles Handy's 'positive steps' for removing causes of blockage in organisational communications (Handy 1988):

- *Use more than one communications network.* Formal communications tend to go through the organisational hierarchy. Other, less formal networks such as peer groups or 'friendship groups' can be used to prepare the environment and to 'underline the formal'.

- *Encourage communications that are two-way.* In two-way 'the recipient is encouraged to intervene in the message to get clarification or to ask questions'. This process can improve both understanding and retention.

- *Keep the links in the communication chain as few as possible.* In this way there is likely to be less distortion of the message.

The following narrative shows the key component parts of the plan and how these may be linked together.

COMPONENT PARTS OF THE HR COMMUNICATION PLAN

The HR communication plan described in Figure 15 provides a framework. It shows a flow chart of a possible approach to developing an HR communication plan. The suggested process relies on segmenting the audiences for the communication (discussed in more detail later), then providing clear messages relevant to each segment. There is an emphasis on important channels of communication, as well as a mechanism for assessing the success of the communication. Note that this is not mandatory, but is by definition to be adapted to each organisation's unique environment. It's important that we don't become preoccupied with the mechanics of the communication plan; instead one must recognise the overall complexity of the process (Timm 1986).

Figure 15 / **The HR communications plan**

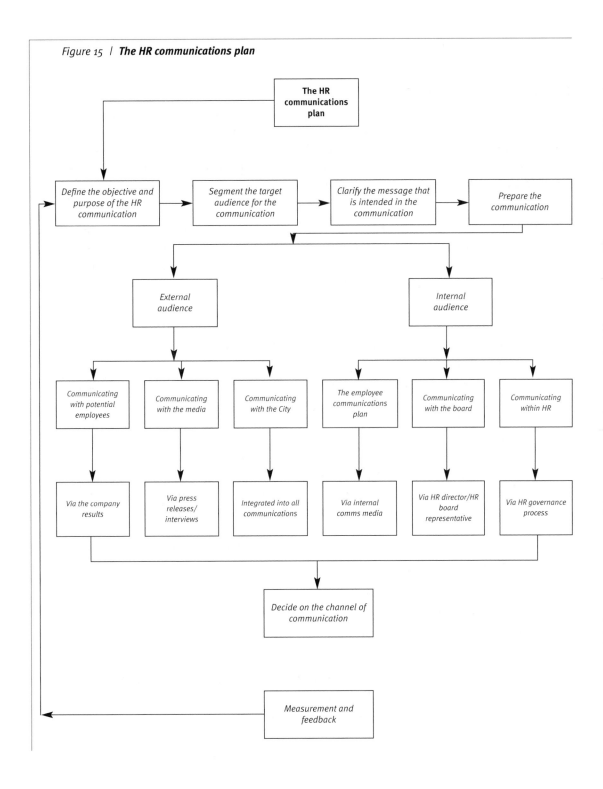

The following section outlines the component parts of the HR communication plan as listed in the diagram.

Purpose of the HR communication

The first thing to be considered for the HR communications plan is its overall purpose. We know that the purpose of the communication can include a variety of objectives, as we saw in the previous chapter. It is likely, though, that the overall purpose will be to convey 'facts, ideas, opinions, beliefs, emotions or motivation' (Blundell 1998). In an organisational sense these generalities are articulated as strategies, plans or change.

There are two aspects to this:

- First, the *preparation of a set of objectives for the whole HR communication plan*. This may be an annual overview taking account of a known set of HR activities. It will be necessary for those in HR to have a full understanding of the business strategy and plans for the year ahead. The overall plan should include:
  - preparation of HR materials for the annual financial reporting season
  - preparation of press releases etc for known significant events – new distribution outlets, closure of manufacturing facilities, outsourcing etc.

- Second, *ensuring that HR is consulted and involved in any significant events* that may not have been foreseen when the original plan was being put together. For example, if a merger or acquisition is announced part-way through a year, HR should have contingencies for dealing with communication demands.

The purpose of the communication can be high-level and strategic – 'to ensure that all employees know their objectives, know what they have to do to achieve them and have sufficient channels to provide feedback on progress against them'. Or it can be more specific – ' to communicate the arrangements for the transition from the company's profit share scheme to a flexible benefits programme'. It is also advisable to have some time-bound targets – 'to communicate the process for e-learning by December 2003'. The purpose or objective for the communication provides the basis on which the communication plan is put together.

A good perspective on this first stage is provided by Bernstein (1984). He raises four questions that should be asked at the beginning of the communication:

- To whom am I speaking?
- What is the value of this communication?
- What is the point or conclusion?
- Can the substance of the whole communication be immediately grasped by the reader through skimming the title or heads and subheads?

These are important fundamentals for each part of the plan.

Segment the audience

It should be clear by now that the target audience for HR communication is not a homogenous one. Let's take, for example, Ethan, a character in Douglas Coupland's book about Generations X and Y, *Microserfs*. Ethan was in his living-room reading copies of *Cellular Buyer's Guide, Dr Dobb's Journal, LAN Times* and *Game Pro*. Now, if you wanted to communicate an important message to Ethan, would you pin a staff notice to the notice-board? Probably not. What we would have to do is devise something specific for Ethan and people like him. But this wouldn't be right for other groups of like-minded individuals. How can the HR communication be dealt with in this scenario? Well, the first thing that those in HR responsible for communication may try is to segment the audience, thereby making targeting of groups for specific messages easier. It may be worth therefore deciding on the 'publics' for the HR communication in much the same way as a marketer would. Examples of these that can be used as guidelines are the 'external' and 'internal' publics.

The external 'publics' for HR communication

It is possible to divide or segment the various parties to be communicated with. In marketing terms these would be known as 'publics'. A marketer would categorise these publics as follows (Kotler and Armstrong 1989):

- *financial publics*. Financial publics influence the company's ability to obtain funds. Banks, investment houses and stockholders are the major financial publics. From an HR perspective this is a relevant segment and one of increasing importance, as we shall see in subsequent chapters.

- *media publics*. Media publics are those that carry news, features and editorial opinion. They include newspapers, magazines and radio and television stations.

- *government publics*. Management takes government developments into account.

- *citizen action publics*. A company's marketing decisions may be questioned by consumer organisations, environmental groups, minority groups and others.

- *local publics*. Every company has local publics such as neighbourhood residents and community organisations.

- *general public*. A company needs to be concerned about the general public's attitude towards its products and activities.

These external publics will form part of the planning process, and understanding what we want to say to them is fundamental.

The internal 'publics' for HR communication

A key part of the HR communication plan is to make sure that the internal 'publics' are effectively targeted. This ensures the most effective deployment of resources and the most appropriate means of communication. The internal segmentation may consist of:

- *employee groups by location*. So, for example, if a particular site has change associated with the business strategy a specific communication campaign should be considered.

- *employee groups by grade*. Again, if there is to be some change associated with HR practice that only applies to certain groups, then they will need some specific, targeted communication.

- *segmentation by demographic category* may also be a useful part of the communication plan.

- *employee groups by trade union or employee representatives*.

What we are trying to do here is to ensure effective targeting of particular groups. This does not mean that general, generic communication will cease, more that it will be complemented by other focused communications.

A segmentation proposal for the HR communication

Figure 15 proposes three key external and three internal communities of interest to whom effective communications need to be directed by those in the HR function. These six elements form part of an integrated approach to communications within HR. A professional approach and detailed understanding of the principles of effective organisational communication should therefore be an integral part of the HR professional's armoury. These have been put forward as a defender, and their importance may vary according to the specific needs of each organisation.

External – the community through the employment brand

The war for talent is with us. It will not go away. Demographic change, social preference and the impact of technology have created an environment where many skills are in short supply across the employment spectrum. If organisations are to meet their own targets for recruiting and retaining the best talent to ensure sustained competitive success, then they will have to communicate their employment advantages to the external market. Employment branding, the use of advance marketing techniques and a greater awareness of the need to be excellent in persuading potential employees that the organisation is right for them means that a professional communications approach to the external community is an essential prerequisite to winning the war for talent (or at least the day-to-day battles). This now falls fairly and squarely within the remit of the HR function. So the HR communication plan should make provision for communicating with the community at large.

The following are some of the things that may be included:

- the development of an employment brand which articulates the values of the organisation as an employer

- national press and PR campaigns about the organisation as an employer

- local press campaigns about the organisation as an employer.

This aspect of HR communication is dealt with in Chapter 8.

External – the City

It has invariably fallen to the chief executive officer and his or her finance director to brief the City about organisational performance. In this respect the City was interested in sales, orders, debtors, stock, cash and a range of ratios (p/e, cost income etc) that demonstrated the organisation's financial performance. However, there is a growing demand for more information about the people in the organisation. Questions range from those about executive succession, pay and the level of training, to pension schemes. In all these there is a growing demand for HR professionals to be aware of and be able to communicate effectively with the City and its analysts.

Some of the components of this part of the HR communication plan may be:

- contributing an HR section to the annual report or developing an annual people report to coincide with the annual results timescales
- making sure that any people aspects of corporate advertising are covered by a professional HR input
- contributing directly or indirectly to the CEO analyst briefings.

Chapter 9 deals with this in more detail.

External – the media

It is increasingly common to see people issues debated in the press, TV or radio. These can vary from the newspaper sales potential of a particularly titillating employment tribunal to the human interest stories surrounding stress in organisations, fat-cat pay, strikes and industrial action, pensions, tax, company cars or the work–life balance – a small selection of recent people issues that have hit the press. Who is the 'front' for these? If a newspaper calls for an interview or a TV reporter requests a short piece on the steps of the town hall, who is the person to whom the organisation will turn for comment? It could be someone from the HR department. So, becoming competent in dealing with the media is an important part of the development of the HR professional.

The final part of the HR plan is to make sure that any communication with the media is done in the most professional way. The following are some of the things that may be included:

- the preparation of press releases on significant people issues
- interviews with reporters from national or local media.

These, then, are some of the things that may be included in the HR communication plan. They are dealt with in more detail in Chapter 10.

Internal – employees

Communicating with and engaging employees is one of the biggest challenges facing organisations today. A challenge that will, in this age of dramatic change, have been felt by anyone who has tried to implement a new customer service strategy, a merger or an organisational change. Quite simply, without the buy-in of employees it is hard to make organisational change work.

There are some basic guidelines to take into account:

- Employees are not a homogenous group. Therefore the mass-market approach to communication may not always be possible (unless it is for something that applies to all – traditionally, the company's annual pay increase or profit share).

- The internal communication plan should take account of the needs of the trade unions or employee representatives. Understanding their position is critical.

- A segmented approach is necessary when communicating. Grade, job type, location and division are obvious segments.

- The channel of communication also needs to be taken into account. It would be easy to assume that everyone has access to the Web, receives mail and gets a briefing from their line manager. Don't assume anything, but research how people prefer to receive any communication that HR may put out.

This is probably the most developed aspect of HR communication (and probably the least effective!). Chapter 11 looks at some of the most important elements of this.

Internal – the board

It was once hardly ever the case that those in HR had board-level accountability. This has changed dramatically. In spite of the brickbats about HR's failure to assert itself at board level, the chances are that many HR functions have to account for their activities and are expected to deliver the 'human' element of strategy. Communicating with the board therefore should be seen as a prime function of those in HR.

There are several ways in which this can be achieved:

- regular HR updates at board meetings

- specific issues-based papers and presentations

- individual briefings on areas of interest.

These are not exclusive, and it is up to those in HR to find out the best route into the board to secure commitment, approval and resource. Chapter 12 deals with this aspect of the HR professional's role in more detail.

Internal – within HR itself

The complexity of HR activity is now so great that joining up the various component parts is critical to the success of the whole. For example, a new reward plan often requires some training, the application of HR technology, integration with recruitment and retention, and effective employee relations. It is no longer (if it ever was) enough to say 'We have a new pay scheme', publish a staff notice and hope that the staff attitude survey will show an improvement in scores in response to the statement 'I am satisfied with my pay.' It is essential to make sure that staff are aware of the scheme, understand it and can access it; that employee representatives and trade unions have been briefed; and that recruiters know how to include it in their 'package'. To achieve this means effective internal communication processes within the HR function – something that should neither be taken for granted nor ignored on the principle that 'It will sort itself out.' Instead, a sophisticated internal communication solution to a complex HR problem is needed.

Communication may be best achieved within HR through:

- *structured HR team meetings* in which each specialist function provides regular updates and reports
- *specific forums* such as the 'HR Strategy Committee', 'the HR Policy Committee' and so on. For those who scorn committees and such formal arrangements, fine. But make sure that there is a systematic process of sign-off, consensus-building and decision-making that takes account of the various stakeholder views within HR.

Ensuring a joined-up approach to HR communication is a critical success factor.

The above description of an approach to segmenting the market for HR communication was put forward as a defender. However, the principle of segmentation is pretty fundamental to the communication process. Segmenting the target audiences in this way allows a better, more focused deployment of resources and messages.

Clarify the message to be communicated

What is it that we are trying to communicate? What is the very essence of the message? It's vital that time is spent on this particular point if success is to be achieved. Munter (1987) has noted that 'too many people simply write or speak in the order that ideas occur to them'; he suggests some important principles, which are:

- Stress the conclusion.
- Divide writing or speaking into main points.
- Subdivide these into supporting points.

It's possible to identify some important yardsticks about communication that apply whether these are in a report, memo or presentation (Vardman and Vardman 1973) as follows:

- Your communication meets a legitimate need for organisational information – ie don't communicate for the sake of it and don't overcommunicate just because you can (usually through the Web)!
- Your communication has a carefully defined purpose – make sure that you understand the reason and objectives behind the communication.
- The receiver is willing and able to understand and respond.
- You employ the proper format.
- The description and evaluation are clearly differentiated.
- The communication is accurate and valid.
- All the above are properly co-ordinated.

These steps are important if the message is to be communicated clearly and appropriately.

Prepare the communication

Preparing the communication can be a nightmare for the HR professional. Unlike some notices about technology or a product, which have single-line ownership, the 'people' communication attracts a vast range of vested interests. These often really are vested – like the CEO, for example! Preparing the communication is therefore a great feat of stakeholder management.

There are several different steps within the preparation phase:

- Decide on the core message.

- Prepare a draft communication.

- Adapt the draft to the channel. It's no use having words that can be easy to read but difficult to speak. Likewise, there may be bandwidth problems on any web-based communication – no graphics, for example.

- Ensure that key stakeholders have a chance to pass comment on the communication.

- Provide tone-of-voice disciplines.

- Ensure that there is a final 'sign-off' process. Is this always the CEO or can a process owner take on this task?

Decide on the right channel for the communication

The previous narrative has shown some of the important principles of communication in its most generic form. However, we have to adapt these principles to make them particularly relevant to the HR applications that we are likely to face. It is important that the right channels of communication are used. In their change programme, DARA, the 2002 *People Management* Award winners, demonstrated this very well. Their strategy involved multidirectional communication, including face-to-face briefings, a regular newsletter, an annual staff survey and use of the company intranet. 'Electronic hubs were set up on the shop floor where the employees would not ordinarily have had access to the intranet' (*People Management* 7 November 2002). This is an excellent example of the point that an HR communication plan should be put in place that uses all relevant channels in its delivery. The model being proposed in this book involves four 'channels' of communication: face to face, telephony, the Web and mail.

The advantages and disadvantages of each of these methods is shown in Table 12. The types of communication within each category include:

Face to face

- line manager briefings

- peer group briefings

- upward feedback

- focus groups

Table 12 | *Advantages and disadvantages of each type of communication channel*

	Advantages	**Disadvantages**
Face to face	• *personalised* • *empathetic* • *allows adaptation for individual circumstances*	• *slow in dispersed sites* • *expensive – productivity lost* • *potential for distortion*
Telephony	• *quick* • *low cost* • *consistent, scripted message*	• *seems impersonal*
Web	• *quick* • *low cost* • *consistent message*	• *inability to recall message once sent is a growing problem for e-mail!*
Mail	• *low cost* • *consistent message* • *generally efficient*	• *slow in dispersed sites* • *may be seen as old fashioned by Generation X!* • *important messages may be lost because of sheer volume of paper sent*

Telephony

- centralised information-gathering
- HR call centres, contact centres or 'helplines'
- upward feedback

Web

- staff notices
- Q&A pages
- upward feedback
- line manager CEO communication

Mail

- staff notice
- individual 'unit of one' communications

These are not the only channels, of course. We've seen the SHRM using radio in the USA and, in some organisations, business TV is also an option. Who knows, with the huge availability of digital channels, the future may see organisations with their own TV channel available in the home. For the time being, though, the above channels are the ones on which we can focus.

Ensure a mechanism for measurement and feedback

We know that every organisation depends on its effective functioning on an 'intricate communication network which has grown up over the years and has proved itself indispensable' (Little 1981). But often this intricacy is based as much on informal as formal communications – which is fine. But how is the feedback from this communication going to get back to those who are trying to decide on the messages, the channels and the types of communication? Here are some ways in which feedback can be obtained:

- Feedback loops on corporate intranet sites can be installed. These may include e-mail addresses or chief executives' webpages with sections for comment; indeed, comment sections can be added to any part of the site.

- Similar types of mechanism can be provided on the Internet sites used by the organisation. External input can also be obtained this way (a good example of this is the CIPD's own websites that have member feedback facilities).

- On team briefings on a particular communication, it could be part of the team leader's job to collate feedback and pass this back through to the communication team or those preparing the communication.

- On paper-based briefings, an attachment could be included to the communication asking for feedback.

Whatever way is used, a collation of information rather than mere anecdote should be sought.

DEVELOPING NEW COMMUNICATION SKILLS FOR THE HR PROFESSIONAL

The HR communication plan and its implementation will not be successful unless those in HR are fully competent in the theory and practice of communication. The following is a description of some of the skills that will be needed.

Developing a communication strategy

This competence will require those in HR to have an understanding of business and HR strategy and design communications interventions that meet the objectives of both. Designing a communications strategy will require a systematic approach with a clear set of objectives and tactics, plans for the optimal use of resources and a set of measurable outcomes. The dependencies of each interlinked part of the communications strategy will be identified and co-ordinated. This strategic approach will require the HR professional to be able to 'helicopter' above the whole organisation, to be able to 'see the bigger picture' and put in place a planned, systematic, proactive communications approach.

Planning and control

Once the communications strategy has been agreed it will be necessary to implement it, with an eye to detail and an understanding of the priorities, tasks, work schedules and resource deployment. In essence the communication strategy is a project that will require the disciplines of project management, and the HR professional will have to have this competence. Clear responsibilities for the various parts of the communication will have to be agreed, articulated and then monitored.

Influencing

A further competence required by the HR professional in his or her communications role will be influencing. It will be necessary to gain the commitment of all the key players to the principles and practice of HR communications. This will not be easy. Time constraints, perceived priorities and managerial apathy (or lack of understanding) may get in the way of effective communication. We all know of the variability of the cascade process, whereby one area can be fully briefed and the next in the dark. The effectiveness of communication will require all the target audiences to have a common understanding, albeit there will be different levels. Influencing the parties to the communications will therefore be a key requirement of the HR professional and is a core competence of the role.

Using information effectively

The final area of competence to be developed by those in HR is an understanding of how to use information effectively. This means finding out exactly what information is required to be communicated, making sure the relevant information is available (ie there are no surprises lurking in the background), and putting forward a balanced view – which is key to professional communication. This is an organisational communication, not political lobbying!

In addition to these competencies there are some areas of personal, generic skill that have to be developed if the HR professional is to achieve success in this communication role. Some of these are as follows:

Personal competencies for the communication role of the HR professional

Oral communication

This means that the HR professional will have to have the ability to exchange information with clear and concise speech that is right for the situation in which the communication is taking place. In many cases this will require the translation of complex messages. The HR professional should therefore be verbally fluent and able to tailor the information to be communicated to the needs of the audience to which it is being addressed.

Written communication

Many organisations use 'tone of voice' techniques for making sure that their communications to customers are written in a language that is friendly, jargon-free and easily understood. The same principles should also apply to HR communication, and the HR professional will need to hone this particular skill for his or her new communication role.

Presentation skills

It is almost certain that the HR professional will find him- or herself in front of an audience of varying size, expected to do the presentation of the communication message. So presentation skills are a necessary competence. This will require the HR professional to be able to present information in a logical and structured way, using a range of presentation techniques appropriate for the audience.

The above are intended as competence guidelines. It will be necessary, though, for the HR professional to enhance and develop his or her competences in several of these areas.

CONCLUSION

Preparing an HR communication plan allows the HR professional to deal with both long- and short-term demands. In the long term the overall purpose of HR communication will be identified and the planning process will facilitate a dialogue about what the key messages or objectives are. Then resources can be allocated to implement the longer-term communication plan. The HR communication plan will also provide a framework within which short-term communication may take place. The benefits of being able to see that next week's pay com- munication coincides with an announcement of a large-scale recruiting or redundancy exercise are great. The absence of such a plan means that HR will not achieve the joined-up approach for which we strive.

Part 3
External communication

8

Communicating with the labour market – using the employment brand

'You're not the man I knew ten years ago.'
'It's not the years, honey, it's the mileage.' Raiders of the Lost Ark (1981)

INTRODUCTION

A lot has changed in the past ten years for HR, particularly when it comes to the external market for labour. We have had to adapt our methods because of the severe shortage of labour. We've made a pretty good job of it in a very tough environment. But are there lessons we can learn in respect of communication? This chapter looks at one particular aspect of this: communicating to the external labour market through the employment brand.

We have an HR communication strategy and an HR communication plan. Now we have to make them work! We have to come up with ideas about how we can achieve the objectives of the strategy by effective communication. This chapter is the first of three about external communication. It deals with how HR might communicate an employment proposition to potential employees and the community at large. Of course, we in HR have been doing this for years. The recruitment process is about communicating with the external labour market and persuading potential employees to join our organisation. So this gives us a head start. Extrapolating from previous methods alone, though, won't be enough. This is because the labour market is different now from what it was before. The upshot is that the need to build a compelling offer of employment has become a priority for employers. To quote one US investment bank, 'We want to stand out in the pack, provide something special in terms of compensation or challenging work' (Corporate Leadership Council 1999).

Now, you may argue that recent banking lay-offs throughout the world have called this approach into question. But, as we know, organisations want to recruit talent whatever the economic climate. The war for talent and the change in the psychological contract have forced a whole new outlook on the working environment – from both sides. Tight employment markets are turning recruitment and retention into priorities for HR functions everywhere. Because of this, great focus is being placed on innovative ways in which employees can be engaged in the organisation. The *employment brand* is one of the methods by which this engagement can be initiated and maintained.

Our key objective here is to become the employer of choice, described by Jon Sparkes as:

> *an employer that the right people choose to work for ... an employer able to satisfy the needs that its employees need to have satisfied by their employer.* Morton *et al* 2002

The employment brand is not a gimmick. It is not a fad that HR has picked up from marketing. Instead it has the potential to be a force for differentiation in a labour market that is more competitive than ever and that shows no sign of easing. Like other marketing activity, marketing for labour through the employment brand should be company-wide, an 'integrating, animating force that binds together other functions rather than subjugating them' (Heller 1988). But why is the development of a marketing approach through employment branding so important?

The war for talent is real

The first reason is that the war for talent has permeated every part of industry, commerce and the public services. This has endured even where there has been an economic downturn. The reason in turn for this is that the war for talent is not specifically related to one industry or geographical sector. It's as hard to get clerical staff in Bristol as it is to get technologists in London. Why is this so? First, it's because there are simply not enough people trained to do the work – the classic case of demand exceeding supply. Second, we have the effect of the demographic change in the labour force. So, it's important to bear in mind that 'people have choices and are attracted to organisations with a strong identity ... to organisations with a sense of purpose' (Arp and Gagneret 2002). The war for talent has increased the need to have effective communication with the labour market.

HR has to engage the community

Belief in the need to communicate effectively with the external labour market means a belief that talent is a scarce resource and that people with talent have to be persuaded to join the organisation. Acceptance of this fundamental point is important. However, there is a wider scale to this than short-term hiring, and this is the second reason for developing an employment brand.

In some communities the role of the employer goes beyond the satisfaction of short-term labour needs. The history of British industry is full of examples of 'industrial towns' where the employer assumed the role of educator, social worker and entertainer. In each community, the employer had a far-reaching social as well as economic role. As this type of model town faded with the various industrial revolutions or recessions of the late twentieth century, employment in these areas seemed more transient. When unemployment was high, there was no need for an employer to build up any sort of rapport with a potential labour force. A job was enough. Things changed as huge demographic changes began to have their effect. The number of vacancies outstripped the number of employees. And this was not only in the south-east of England. Many parts of the UK experienced labour shortages in several different occupations.

The rules changed. First came the price wars, where call centres competed with each other in gaining the labour of an employee. In some parts of the UK, a few hundred pounds was sufficient to persuade an employee to move from one company to another. But even this soon became a difficult model to sustain. And so the employer as a member of the community was an idea that came back into fashion. The initial push for this was economic. But this has coincided with a new view of how organisations should present themselves to the public. An economic necessity – to present a good employment image to the community – has therefore converged with a social imperative – to be a responsible organisation. It is very likely that HR will lead the first. It is possible that they will be involved in the second. The employer brand is a way of combining the attributes necessary to secure a good image in *both* areas.

Organisations need to articulate their values

The third reason for developing an employer brand also concerns the way organisations represent themselves to their employees and the public. We've probably all read the pundit's view of the future workplace and its role in society. We probably have our own opinions of these views. However, there is a subject that seems to be getting more than its fair share of debate: the role of the organisation in an increasingly globalised world. Naomi Klein's book *No Logo* is certainly high on the *Zeitgeist*-ometer. Its chapter headings (eg 'Brand Bombing', Corporate Censorship', 'Breeding Disloyalty') paint a very different picture from the cheerleader mentality of the traditional corporate history. Its conclusion that globalisation has created the need for some common standards – not yet provided by governments – has contributed hugely to the globalisation debate. Solutions have been offered. Some will get taken up. But, whether we agree or disagree with Klein's sentiment, there is a growing need for organisations to state what they are about – to define their values and just where they stand. To borrow the title of Moynagh and Worsley's book, in 'tomorrow's workplace' organisations will have to be more explicit about their values and will be obsessed with their reputation: 'The gap between consumer values and the values of the organisation imposes additional costs. Narrowing the gap has become a management priority' (Moynagh and Worsley 2001). Those in HR have a role to play in determining exactly what these values are and how they are communicated to the external community.

So there is a compelling case for the organisation to make its values known in its external communication. These values are no longer just about product or service but about employment and social responsibility. The employment brand is one way of encapsulating these values.

WHAT IS AN EMPLOYMENT BRAND?

One definition of the employment brand is something

> *built upon the specific job offers that a firm provides to its current and potential employees ... the term 'job offer' or 'employment offer' refers to the employment value proposition a firm makes to its recruits through specific job offers, as well as the day offer or relationship a firm provides to its current employees – the offer that holds them to the firm.* Corporate Leadership Council 1999

An employment brand is a derivative of the overall brand of the organisation. In this context a brand has been defined as 'a name, term, sign, symbol or design, or a combination of them, intended to identify the goods or services of one seller or group of sellers and to differentiate them from those of competitors' (Kotler and Armstrong 1989). It serves a number of purposes (Clutterbuck and Dearlove 1993):

- differentiation in the marketplace
- high visibility
- image enhancement
- consistency of message
- creation of a sense of ownership among those involved with the brand
- product association
- reputation reinforcement
- continuity, because the brand has an intrinsic value, independent of particular product or service offerings.

These principles are adhered to when marketers develop a product or service brand. When branding works in a marketplace it is a powerful differentiator and can contribute greatly to an organisation's success. For example, the top US brand leaders in 1923 were Campbell's Soup and Coca Cola. The top UK brands in 1933 were Brooke Bond tea, Cadbury's chocolate and Colgate toothpaste (Macrae 1991). These brands still retain leadership positions. There are several types of corporate brand that are used in different ways. Often there will be variations between parent organisation and subsidiary. Figure 16 demonstrates this. The figure shows that there can be numerous types of corporate identity, depending on the nature of the organisation. The figure represents several possibilities:

- A dominant parent organisation that may want to ensure that the business brand, and hence the employment brand, applies to all HR materials.
- If there is a diversified company, and hence no single identity as reflected in the brand, there will be the issue of how (or whether) to 'enforce' an employment brand on the subsidiary brands.

The challenge in a multibranded organisation is to ensure that the employment brand is applicable across all brands. Van Riel (1992) has concluded that where there is uniformity, 'tight guidelines with respect to communication are imposed from the top of the organisation'. There is no ambiguity about the overall brand or the employment brand. In those organisations where there is a variety of brands the situation is more difficult to manage. The subsidiaries may want to maintain their distinctiveness and therefore be reluctant to 'join in' with the employment branding campaign. In some circumstances, this will be OK. For example, in the 'finance-oriented corporate identity' in Figure 16 this will often refer to the 'conglomerate' of organisations where financial return is the real link. As such, there is still a case for employment branding at the corporate level, but it is not as strong. Each case will be taken on its merit.

The principles of strong brand association and corporate success can be equally applicable when developing a brand to attract potential employees. In this respect the 'product' is the employment attributes of the company. These might include:

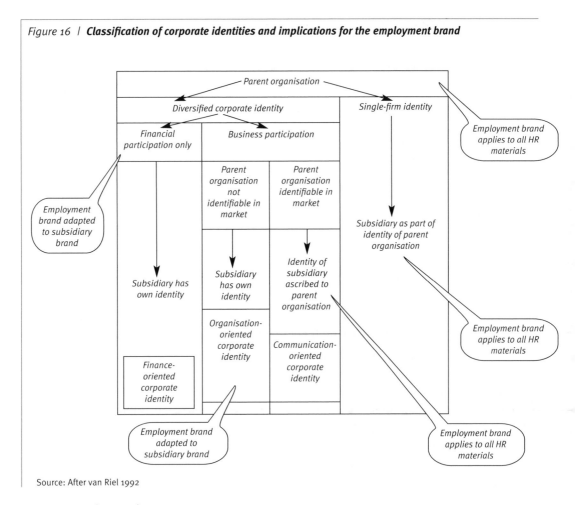

Figure 16 / **Classification of corporate identities and implications for the employment brand**

Source: After van Riel 1992

- pay and reward
- training and development
- quality reputation
- career opportunity
- work–life balance
- diversity reputation.

A more comprehensive list of these attributes is included in Table 13. In this analysis the Corporate Leadership Council (1999), using references from 19 major US organisations, has articulated some of the attributes that may attract potential employees and hence are worth emphasising in an employment proposition. Recent research, again carried out by the Corporate Leadership Council (2002), has updated this compelling offer. Some of the key findings were that, *inter alia*, pay and reward remained the most critical factor, but that manager quality, hours worked and job fit remained high on the list.

Table 13 | The compelling job offer:the offers a firm makes to the labour market Job offer components/dimensions

Work–life balance	Company culture/ environment	Product/company strength	Compensation and benefits	Work environment
Business travel	Senior team	Reputation	Salary	Manager quality
Location	quality		External equity	Co-worker quality
Flexitime	Development		Internal equity	Recognition
Childcare	Reputation		Bonus	Empowerment
Work hours	Technology level		Stock options	Work challenge
Vacation	Risk-taking		Retirement	Cutting-edge work
Telecommuting	Environment		Contributions	Internal mobility
	Company fit		Health benefits	Role clarity
	Company size			Project responsibility

Source: Corporate Leadership Council 1999

The employment brand will seek to articulate these in a way that can be understood by potential employees and make it attractive for them to think about working for the organisation.

This is the starting point for trying to work out what an employment brand is and how it is derived. But what exactly does an employment brand include? Well, first and foremost it is an extension of the organisation's overall brand. It is rarely a stand-alone or sub-brand. Second, it is used to embrace and articulate the values of the organisation as an employer to existing or potential employees. (This chapter deals with the latter.)

Given the above description, is it possible to highlight the characteristics of actual employment branding when it hits the street? We can do this by looking at how organisations have extended their product or service brands to deal with the need to be perceived as attractive to potential employees.

EXAMPLES OF EMPLOYMENT BRANDING

So what employment brands exist today? And can we see from them that they have embraced the principles outlined above? In some organisations the employment brand is a clearly adapted variation of the product brand. For example, Lloyds TSB uses 'Your life, your career, your bank' to complement its corporate brand when dealing with HR issues. This employment brand was developed in 2000 and mirrored a new brand campaign that was taking place within the organisation as a whole. It was used on internal documents issued to staff and on external recruitment literature. More recently it has been used in graduate recruitment and can be seen on the corporate website. Each aspect of the employment proposition – 'Your life, your career, your bank' – has a specific set of values and associated services on offer to the potential recruit.

There are other examples. The London Borough of Newham advertises vacancies with the slogan 'Opportunities for the best in local government'. This was an advertisement for HR professionals that emphasised career opportunity. Wolverhampton City Council emphasised diversity with its 'Putting equal opportunities into action'. A similar stance was taken by the National Crime Squad with their 'Driving diversity forward'. Each of these has taken the overall organisational brand and added to it an attractive proposition in respect of the human element of the organisation.

There were some brilliant instances at the 2002 Recruitment Marketing Awards of how organisations were using employment branding in a variety of forms to attract labour. The Grand Prix winner, for example, was the London Fire Brigade. The description of the advertisement noted that 'this was not only about filling vacancies: it also sent out a message about the culture and values of the organisation' (*People Management* 27 June 2002). This is a perfect example of how a particular organisation wanted to send the message to the employment market that it encouraged diversity in its workforce and therefore would welcome applicants from a variety of backgrounds. The advertisement did this in a subtle and intelligent yet straightforward way. All were the characteristics of excellent employment branding.

Other winners included the Metropolitan Police, whose slogan was 'Most employers will give you a salary every month ... what else?' In this approach it was noted that the advert 'tackled a serious issue for school and college leavers considering a career in the police service: pay'. In the Sainsbury's advertisement 'The only thing we label is our food,' the message was about diversity. Dianah Worman of the CIPD said of it, 'This advert is not just about targeting one particular minority group. Diversity advertising is increasingly about the overall aim of finding talents and skills from all parts of the labour market, however diverse, rather than attracting one specific group' (*People Management* 27 June 2002).

In these examples the organisations used the opportunity of a simple objective – recruitment – to portray their cultural facets and values. They did this because they recognised that potential employees in the twenty-first century want to know what it would be like to work for them, as well as the specific characteristics of the job. To tell them meant that these organisations had to come up with innovative approaches to their employment branding.

PRINCIPLES FOR PREPARING AN EMPLOYMENT BRAND

From these examples and other research, what can we conclude as important principles to bear in mind when preparing an employment brand? What we are trying to do here is to develop a compelling offer to the labour market that differentiates our organisation from others. We can of course refer here to the experience of the marketing professionals in their broad knowledge of branding over many years (see Kotler and Armstrong 1989). Macrae (1993), for example, highlights sources for marketing brand visibility that include 'product capabilities, marketing edge, star identity and image bonds'.

Not all of these will be relevant in the employment brand, but some of the principles can be applied. So, pulling all this together, what might we conclude are the characteristics of the employment brand?

- First, the brand should help 'the buyer' to make the decision. In employment branding the name, term or symbol should clearly identify and differentiate the employment opportunity with the organisation from those of competitors in the labour market. 'We recruit policemen' would not satisfy the criteria. The Metropolitan Police advertisement above would!

- Second, the employment brand should say something about the quality of the opportunity that the employer has to offer. In the London Ambulance Service advertisements (finalists at the Recruitment Marketing Awards 2002), dramatic slogans such as '**** off, I want to die' and 'Am I going to lose my baby?' were used to demonstrate the overall theme of the advertisement, which was 'It's not an everyday job.' The quality of this advert was embedded in the nature of the job itself: one of a valuable, life-saving part of the community. It would be difficult to imagine a greater quality of job than that.

- Third, there is the question of consistency of 'purchase' associated with the employment brand. In traditional labour market recruitment, it was possible to see several parts of the organisation, with slightly different job requirements advertising in the same media at the same time. How must a potential employee feel about this organisation, when there is some of the imaginative employment branding highlighted in the above examples? A better approach is consistency of culture and value message in the employment branding campaign.

These principles should at least give a general idea of the kind of things embraced in employment branding. From these it is possible to develop a checklist that will help in preparing the brand itself.

DEVELOPING AN EMPLOYMENT BRAND

The development of an employment brand will come about because the organisation has recognised that the market for labour is tough and getting tougher. It is no longer enough to assume that potential employees will want 'a job'. They will, of course, but there are other factors that they will take into account. The most important of these are about the organisation as a place to work as reflected by its culture and values. Now, these are actually quite difficult to articulate. So a process should be undertaken that facilitates the definition of what exactly goes into the employment brand and how it is communicated to the labour market. In this respect developing the employment brand is akin to 'applying market principles to HR'. Some of these might be to (Corporate Leadership Council 1999):

- focus on corporate strategic goals and objectives – which will ultimately determine the organisation's marketing strategy

- use market research in order to understand fully the customer – which in this case is the employee or potential employee

- design a compelling set of HR products and services – ie those that 'meet customer preferences'

- build and enhance the brand over a period of time.

Figure 17 | ***Labour market segmentation***

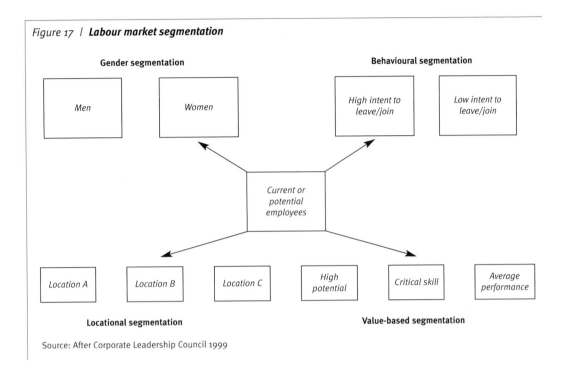

Source: After Corporate Leadership Council 1999

The fundamental principle by which we are designing an employment brand is to build a compelling offer from or an employment values proposition for the organisation. Research by the Corporate Leadership Council (1999) has shown that the values and preferences of employees or potential employees included, amongst other things, compensation and benefits ('confirming conventional wisdom'), the work environment, the work–life balance and the organisational environment. Here, therefore, is a checklist to work through:

- *Establish the values and preferences of potential employees*
  In parallel with our deciding, from an internal perspective, what the good things about our company are, we should also research the market against other potential employers. This will allow us to identify those parts of the organisation – with particular reference to working for the organisation – that are different. We should then establish what the preferences of potential employees are. These may include pay but are almost certain to include such things as employment opportunity and career development. There is a raft of fairly obvious things that we shall be able to identify. Of course, we should not ignore the less obvious. Ethical behaviour, environmental awareness and customer perceptions are increasingly important factors in deciding where to work.

- *Articulate these in meaningful and easy-to-understand language, ie develop an employment brand that combines the key differentiators into a compelling offer*
  Having identified the key differentiators of our organisation from those of our competitors for a particular labour pool, we now want to articulate them in a way that

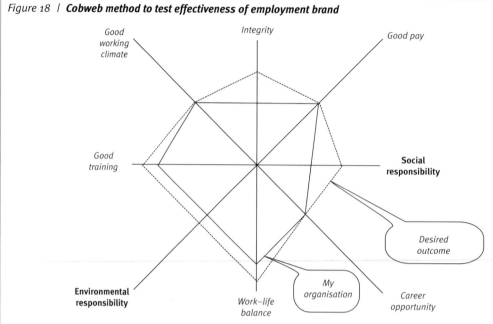

Figure 18 | Cobweb method to test effectiveness of employment brand

Source: After van Riel 1992

can be communicated effectively. When Avis wanted to market their own services they came up with the brand 'We are number two – we try harder.' This was a simple and brilliant way of communicating what the customer might expect from the organisation. What we have to do in HR is to take this principle and use it in the employment brand. In effect we are 'marketing the job offer like a product to build a stronger brand' (Corporate Leadership Council 1999).

- *Market-test the employment proposition with employees or potential employees*
  An option at this point is to take soundings about how potential or actual employees view the employment brand once it is developed. A straightforward way is to run some focus groups and have an overt market test. However, there may be other ways that can draw on existing HR information. Staff attitude surveys, for example, can be a rich source of information about the things that employees see as priorities. In addition some organisations do research on 'Why did you join the organisation?' Braver ones do research on 'Why did you leave the organisation?' as well.

- *Ensure that the employment brand is integrated into all published materials*
  Now comes the hard bit for the HR function: implementation. Because employment branding is likely to be an innovative approach for many organisations, a significant selling job (also known as stakeholder management) will be needed. The first group will be those within HR itself. The challenge will be to make sure that all recruitment, training, reward and employee materials that go public include the employment brand concept as part of their design. Then those in HR will have to persuade

everyone associated with employee or potential employee communication that the branding concept is a good one and can help. We have to make sure that it is consistently applied over time. A brand will not always have an immediate impact: it takes time to become established. This will require HR professionals to become brand managers in a deliberate and systematic way, establishing 'consumer' awareness, making sure that the brand has value, making sure that it is actually helping to differentiate and so on.

- *Target the brand effectively to employee 'segments' (see Figure 17 for examples of employee segments)*
  If we believe that the employment branding concept will work, then we might as well adopt another marketing tool: segmentation. In Figure 17 various ways of dividing potential employees into groups with shared preferences is shown. This can be used only so far, in that the employment brand is intended to be pretty universal. However, its main use may be in the distribution of the brand, ie having a more focused set of campaigns for each segment, instead of the blunderbuss approach to recruitment.

- *Market the job offer like a product to a customer*
  It goes without saying that the principles of employment branding and segmentation are intended to provide a different way of reaching the awareness of potential employees. Indeed, we can go as far as to say that 'employment' with the organisation is the product and potential employees are customers of the organisation. The mindset to achieve this is more akin to that of the marketer than the HR professional – but here is an area where the two converge.

  - *Measure effectiveness*
  Finally, as in any other brand campaign, we should measure the effectiveness of the proposition. The ultimate measure is if we are able to fill the quota of recruits needed by the organisation. After all, this is the basic underlying objective of the whole activity, although retention may also benefit. There are other things that can be done, too: brand awareness within the market segments, before-and-after measures, and so on. A useful and simple method for examining the value of the employment brand and its effectiveness is the 'cobweb method', often used in marketing for a variety of analytical processes. Figure 18 shows how this might be adapted to apply to employment branding. In this the values included in the employment brand are shown at the extremities of each strand of the cobweb. A desired outcome (determined by benchmarking) is set and a comparison with the current state of play (determined by employee research) is used to show how close the match is. It's possible to use this to set targets.

PACKAGING THE EMPLOYMENT BRAND

Having come up with a brand likely to articulate the values and culture of the organisation in a way attractive to potential employees (and helpful for retaining current employees), you need to consider the issue of 'packaging'. Packaging is 'the methodology for putting the organisation's products and services across' (Thomson 1990).

There are a number of media that might be included in packaging, and these should be 'employment-branded' if appropriate. A good example of this was mentioned earlier in the Lloyds TSB graduate recruitment website with the employment brand 'Your life, your career, your bank' shown prominently on first entry to the site.

Here are some other areas of packaging that could be included (Thomson 1990):

- *Paper-based*
  Letters and memos
  Headed paper for people issues
  Posters
  Reports
  Manuals
  Magazines and newspapers
  Certificates
  Brochures
  Mailshots

- *Visual material*
  PowerPoint® presentations
  Overheads
  Flipcharts

- *Computer-based*
  E-mail
  Websites
  Screensavers

The employment brand can be incorporated into any material used to express the organisation's values for the purposes of attracting potential employees. It is very necessary for someone in HR to have responsibility for ensuring that the employment brand is presented consistently – often a weakness in the management of HR's communication portfolio.

DISTRIBUTING THE EMPLOYMENT BRAND

Having decided on an employment brand and then ensured that it was included in important internal and external materials through well-monitored packaging, you now face the question of distribution: how to get the brand to its target audience of potential employees? Again, some basic marketing principles apply here.

Philip Kotler (1986) has noted that 'a marketing channel performs the work of moving goods from producers to consumers'. The employment brand is a way of advertising the organisation's employment proposition and needs to be communicated via the appropriate channels into the labour market. It is important to maximise the value of the employment brand once developed. This is achieved by making sure it is incorporated into all the materials made public about the organisation's employment proposition:

- through the media, by incorporating the employment brand into advertising and public relations materials

- through the Web, by making sure the employment brand is featured as part of the organisation's 'e' offering

- by agreeing with the organisation's preferred recruitment agencies that the employment brand becomes an integral part of the employment offer and marketing campaigns.

The above would seem pretty straightforward – but it isn't. First of all, we have to make sure that all the functions of HR that have any contact with the labour market understand and buy into the concept of employment branding and then incorporate the brand into their own materials. Second, we have to ensure consistency of approach, ie that sub-brands don't start to appear within HR and that each and every advert has the brand included. Third, we have to make sure that when line managers are discussing employment prospects, they too are aware of and use the employment brand's key themes.

CONCLUSION

Marketing and branding have not traditionally been on the radar for the HR professional. Over the years various people have tried to instil a market/customer-based approach into the HR function, and this has definitely had some success. HR professionals are far more aware nowadays of the need to be 'customer-facing' in all that they do. One group of customers is potential employees. The employment brand is a way of professionally communicating with this group.

In designing brands unique to the HR profession we are taking a step function, treading new ground. This requires the acquisition of new skills and professional advice from those who know about marketing issues, ie marketing professionals. A good working relationship with the organisation's brand experts would not go amiss as the process is developed.

9

HR's role in communicating with the City

We accept the reality of the world with which we are presented. The Truman Show (1998)

INTRODUCTION

The share price of an organisation can move significantly based on reports in the press, briefings given to analysts or buying (and selling) on the part of a pension fund. Mostly the reasons for this are financial: profit or loss anticipation, forecast changes in cost–income ratio or a proposed rights issue. However, there is evidence that financial stakeholders are increasingly interested in issues of human capital when making their buy/sell/hold decisions about an organisation. Investors require that the communication from the CEO exhibit the qualities of credibility, efficacy, commitment and responsibility (Segars and Kohut 2001). More and more these qualities require information about the organisation's human resources as well as its financial ones. This in turn requires that those in HR take a very active role in this communication process with the City and financial stakeholders. There are principles of communication here that can also be used in those organisations that don't report to the City: for example, what information HR should be communicating to the external marketplace. The scope, then, of this chapter is wide.

For the purposes of deciding how HR professionals should be involved in supporting City communications I have taken a definition that is broader than 'the stockbrokers and market-makers of the Square Mile'. For the purposes of this chapter, the City includes (Smith 1989):

- self-investing institutions (eg pension funds)
- fund management groups (eg merchant banks and investment companies)
- stockbroking firms (or those whose role involves the making of markets)
- merchant banks
- employee shareholders
- private investors
- the financial media.

The attention being paid to how organisations deal with investors is assuming a new level of importance (Coyne and Witter 2002). There is a realisation that one size does not fit all, and that the City and its investors require different types of information depending on their strategic positioning (ie the things they regard as important to the success of the company).

A recent analysis identified three different types of investor. One is the *organisation maven*, who focuses exclusively on organisational issues. Such investors may sell or buy shares after examining a company's measures for training front-line management or following a change in senior management. The second type is the *strategy junkie*. The third is the *financial addict*. It is the first of these, the organisation maven, to which greater HR focus should be devoted.

This observation is also recognised by those who invest, and recommend that others invest, in the organisation. Collectively these people can be termed 'the City'. We know that the appointment of an individual 'star' can add millions to the value of an organisation. (For example, when Stella McCartney joined Chloe, sales were reported to have gone up by 400 per cent.) But I wonder if there will be greater recognition of the totality of the organisation's people management policies and practices in future. If so, it is up to those in HR to understand the particular interests of the City as a whole and be able to communicate information that adds value to the overall perception of the organisation by those who wish to invest in it.

BUT WHAT DOES THE CITY *DO*?

The City is the collective term used for a square mile of London (and Canary Wharf) in which a huge volume of financial transactions takes place. In any one day some £50 billion of foreign currency is traded, in addition to the stocks and shares of the 'Footsie' (FTSE – the Financial Times Stock Exchange 100 share index) and the huge market for bonds. Furthermore, London is the world's 'most important centre for investment banking, commercial law and international accountancy' (Chapman 1991). In short, the City is a huge financial market in which buyers (individuals, companies, pension funds and governments) and sellers (same list) are brought together, backed up by administrative and regulatory frameworks. Similar financial markets exist in many other major cities, including New York (Wall Street), Tokyo, Paris and Frankfurt.

What kind of material is relevant to this group of people? Written materials include (Smith 1989):

- the annual report
- the interim report
- special offers to shareholders
- financial advertising
- annual report advertising
- corporate advertising.

I've taken the liberty of including a wide range of financial interests under the definition of the single term, 'the City'. Whilst this is not strictly accurate, it does give us a shorthand way of covering an interest group of growing importance to HR.

HR AND THE CITY

In today's commercial environment the value of an organisation is increasingly dependent on such intangible assets as people. Communicating the specific value of the people assets to the City is therefore a priority. The new focus on human capital management and measurement will sharpen HR's involvement with the City. Key findings of a recent report showed that:

- certain large investors believe there is a link between human capital activities and shareholder value

- the majority of HR professionals do not collaborate with finance or strategy colleagues when they design human capital measures

- few companies release human capital measures, owing to fear of releasing competitor-sensitive information.

It's clear that if HR are going to deliver their part of the bargain in enhancing the human capital value of the organisation, then the function will have to develop new ways of communicating this information to the City.

A GREATER INTEREST IN 'PEOPLE ISSUES' BY THE CITY

Once the sole province of the finance director, there is a growing awareness that other information, including that related to 'people', is of interest to and should be communicated to the financial stakeholders. This chapter outlines some things that may be relevant to HR's communications with the City.

The growing interest in 'people' and their effect on the financial performance of an organisation's stock means that those in HR are likely to have to understand, provide information on and have a plan for dealing with such issues as they pertain to the City and other financial stakeholders. Actually, its decision has been made for us. The Accounting Standards Board reported in 2002, recommending a new approach to the operating and financial review of the organisation. Amongst its recommendations were that the OFR (operating and financial review) should discuss qualitative factors as well as quantitative ones. Such factors could be skills shortages and health and safety matters (Accounting Standards Board 2002). The OFR should discuss the objectives of the business and how exactly the managers of the company are going to deliver these objectives through their business strategy. In particular it was recommended that amongst the issues for comment, intellectual capital and its 'potential impact on performance' should be raised. Furthermore, the Council for Excellence in Management and Leadership report, *Measuring Corporate Management and Leadership*, presented the case for corporate reporting and concluded that 'greater corporate reporting and disclosure in the field of organisational management and leadership is not only desirable but inevitable' (Neely, Gray, Kennerley and Marr 2001).

We're on new ground here. The tick-box approach to the HR contribution to the annual reporting season seems to be disappearing fast. It would seem that the need to present relevant, value-adding information about the organisation's human capital, as well as its financial capital, is now with us. Those responsible for HR communication will have to be able to respond to this new challenge by effective understanding of the needs of the City and financial stakeholders, and by providing information that satisfies these needs. Some have already recognised this. A rennet report about Barclay's bank in the UK noted that 'around 50 front-line staff will be on hand to answer investors' and analysts' questions and to demonstrate the quality of the organisation's people' (Arkin 2002).

In addition there are also tactical communication requirements in relation to the interest of the City in HR issues. These may arise from several sources:

- The appointment of a new CEO or board director inevitably causes a stir in stock market dealers and commentators. There is a role for those in HR in putting together appropriate PR materials to go as part of a press pack or release.

- The announcement of a merger or acquisition raises a good deal of interest in the City, mostly about cost reduction or revenue growth. However, the growing recognition that such ventures fail because of the personalities involved means that a good deal of interest is shown in the people involved. Those in HR should be proactive in raising and providing information to a broader PR programme about this particular aspect.

- The announcement of increases in jobs through, say, the opening of new retail outlets creates interest in the City. HR again should be proactive in preparing relevant information.

- The announcement of job cuts has City repercussions that require a professional HR input.

Each of these scenarios generates City interest and can affect the share price of the organisation. In the past they have tended to take second place to other information of a purely financial nature. The recognition of the people factor in share price and company valuation movements means however that those in HR are likely to play a more proactive role in future and should prepare accordingly.

Other areas where HR professionals may be dealing with financial stakeholders are:

- at the *annual general meeting* (AGM), where inevitably there will be people-related questions from shareholders. HR will have a major role in either briefing the chair or CEO of the organisation on possible answers or in taking questions directly from the platform.

- in the *annual report*, where traditionally the HR role has been to provide remuneration information about directors. Now there may well be a growing interest in other people-related matters: pensions, turnover, training investment and so on.

- in *event-based people issues*, such as the appointment of a new director, where the City may take an interest. Those in HR will be asked, increasingly, to get involved with the press release.

What all of these things mean is that HR professionals have to hone their communication skills when it comes to dealing with the City and other financial stakeholders in the organisation. In the past, though, there may not have been too much contact with analysts, and the closest many people in HR may have been to the City was through their business studies qualifications (or through watching *Sex and the City*!). There simply hasn't been the need. HR professionals dealt with 'the people'. The chief executive officer and the finance director were the ones who dealt with the organisation's shareholders and with the City as the market for those shares. All this is changing, though, as greater focus is placed on people as critical factors in sustained organisational success.

WHAT HR MATTERS INTEREST THE CITY?

We have all heard of City matters. Throughout the 1980s the City was associated with extremes of wealth, huge bonuses and a massive amount of press coverage – junk bond dealing, mergers and acquisitions, *Barbarians at the Gate* and *Wall Street*. But underneath all this the period saw 'more fundamental changes in finance and investment than any similar period since the Great Depression' (Downes and Goodman 1991). 'The City', embracing so many of the world's financial transactions, provided the oil on which industry and commerce run. The 1990s also had its headline incidents (Baring's Bank stands out), but greater regulation has lessened the chances of such extremes and a greater focus on risk management has sharpened a prudence that was already present in most financial institutions.

It is this greater focus on the inside management of the organisation that means HR will in future have to be effective in communicating to this new audience of company watchers who make buy-and-sell decisions on their perception of how good an organisation's prospects are. One of these prospects is the organisation's people management.

WHAT METRICS CAN HR COMMUNICATE TO THE CITY?

The greater emphasis on the importance of HR metrics to the internal running of the organis-ation has now manifested itself in the external presentation of information, as we have seen. It has been noted that 'HR is facing such an increased pressure to demonstrate accountability for human capital to the business and the CEO that effective HR metrics have become imperative' (Corporate Leadership Council 2002).

It is possible to identify three types of HR metrics that would be of interest to the City (Corporate Leadership Council 2002):

- *Strategic alignment*
  This would show how the organisation's HR policies, practices and strategies are aligned with the business strategy. Of particular interest to the City would be succession plans for board members, reward and industrial relations strategies that are consistent with the business objectives, and so on. Furthermore, where a merger and acquisition (M&A) or international expansion is proposed as part of the strategy presented to the City and other stakeholders, they will ask, 'Is this organisation capable of delivering this strategy? Does it have the skill to do a major M&A strategy?' The answer to the question could affect the value of the organisation on the market.

- *Value-based return on investment*
  As we move towards better ROI (return on investment) approaches to HR activities, these will become of interest. Of course the most obvious VBROI is director's pay. The organisation's remuneration committee will have applied their own rigorous criteria to the value of the reward package for the senior directors, and this will already have been reported in the annual reporting process. However, it's likely that other values-based measures will be included in future. An example would be the return on investment from training. Currently (let's say) the board of directors takes a particular interest in training. Has investment gone up during the year? Do we spend more than our competitors on training? Once the ROI model has been demonstrated more effectively in training, and a measured increase in shareholder value can be shown by such investment, then this will be of interest to the City.

- *'Ongoing metrics process improvement'*
  As HR metrics start to be reported in depth to the City, comparators will be made over time. Productivity improvements and cost–income ratios will be compared with previous years' and with other organisations'. There will be a greater responsibility on the part of management to demonstrate improvements, and the HR community will be tasked with coming up with ways these might be achieved.

The current debate about human capital has heightened the awareness of the need for better HR metrics in a general sense. This coincides with a greater interest on the City's part in measuring the effectiveness of HR activities as they impinge on the value of the organisation.

But how should this valuable information be reported?

SOME KEY PRINCIPLES FOR COMMUNICATING WITH 'THE CITY'

There are some important principles to bear in mind when communicating with the City. Gummer (1987) has outlined these in a financial sense. However, I believe they are just as important in HR communication with the City.

So what are the principles, and how should HR respond? When establishing a policy for a public company's communication programme with the City, it is important that the public company adheres to the following three principles:

- *The City hates surprises*. What kind of surprises might we have up our sleeve that relate to HR issues? Well, the first and most obvious is a downsizing programme. It is always a difficult decision to communicate this. Some believe it implies some kind of failure on the part of the organisation to manage its resources. Yet this is not always the case. Often market forces, technological developments or other extraneous factors can affect an organisation's manpower plan. Recognition of the fact that downsizing has to be part of the cost control or resource redeployment – however unfortunate this is – is actually a sign of proactive management. The issue is often one of timing: when to go to market and when not to. Those responsible for HR should have a key role to play here:

- first, in making sure that employees' representatives and trade unions are consulted about the downsizing before it goes public

- second, in making sure that employees know about it – there is nothing worse than their reading about the downsizing in the press before they themselves have been told

- third, in making sure that the words used in the communication are the right ones, that take into account any efforts at redeployment, and that they are not just cold, factual, actuarial statements.

- *A public company must be prepared to share both the good news and the bad.* This again relates to the first point above. Even though this is an obvious statement it still requires careful thought in its implementation. More than anything, timing is the issue here, and HR professionals have a duty of care to make sure that all the loose ends have been tied before the bad news goes to the City. As importantly, the presentation of good news – job creation, pay increases, bonus awards – can backfire if not well thought through with HR input. Again, reading about good news first in the press can be counterproductive. It's all about keeping the employee informed as well as the City.

- *It is only very rarely that public companies get away with being less than honest with the City.* Need we dwell on this point? It is vital that HR issues are presented to the City in a way that is honest and true. Trying to put a misleading spin on a piece of news – HR 'news' included – is always bad.

These principles apply as much to those in HR who are supporting a broader PR programme with the City than any other function. How does this manifest itself?

HOW SHOULD HR COMMUNICATE WITH THE CITY?

There is no right way to prepare a communication plan with the City. But there are some principles to consider. In the first instance, it is unlikely that HR would communicate separately. In almost every scenario the HR element is part of a wider, financially based briefing. Those in HR, though, should make sure that they are consulted before the communication happens. We have to work hard to achieve this. It is not a natural part of City-based financial communication to include HR matters – but it is a growing area of interest.

Second, there should be an overall plan for the corporate communication of which an HR element is to be included. The following is adapted from a guide to effective corporate communications. The basis of this is a ten-step plan for corporate communication (Weford 1987) that has been put into an HR context:

Step 1 Understand the business objectives and strategy

In HR terms this means making sure that the human implications of the strategy *and* their likely impact on the organisation's value as perceived by the City is understood and communicated. The opening of 100 new retail outlets, the expansion into Europe, the opening of a factory in

China, the closure of a dot.com subsidiary – all of these have human implications. It is imperative that those in HR are part of the strategic process and have an input accordingly.

Step 2 Agree realistic communications objectives

In a broader sense, an objective might be ' to persuade the City that the opening of new retail outlets is a sign of a prosperous, well-managed and successful growth strategy'. This means that jobs will be created. The HR sub-objective may be to present this positively so that recruitment into these is easier. Communicating with the City won't affect this directly, but it will lead to a greater awareness of the plans that will inevitably filter through to the labour market.

Step 3 Understand your target audiences

Who is the target audience for HR communication in the context of the City? Well, all shareholders will be interested in what is happening to the people. It's up to HR to understand the needs of City audiences. What do analysts want to know about the organisation's human capital? What do pension fund buyers want to know about the organisation's plans for its manpower? Those in HR will become increasingly involved in such dialogue – indeed, many already are – and therefore an understanding of the audience is important.

Step 4 Develop an intelligence system

In HR terms this means trying to spot the things likely to cause a buzz in any City communication. Anything associated with pensions or pension fund provisions is of interest, for example. A good check on how investors are analysing companies can be gleaned from such publications as *Company Reporting*, which is about 'improving standards of financial reporting practice', In issue 141, March 2002, for example, share options and pensions in particular were under the spotlight. Previous issues included items on intangible assets and the change in the numbers of employees in organisations. It is clear that people issues, once a below-the-line issue for investors, are now well above the line. Those in HR should take an increasingly proactive role in this and they will therefore need an intelligence system about what is likely to be of interest and what the organisation is likely to communicate to the City.

Step 5 Establish priorities for target audiences

It goes without saying that some HR issues will be more important than others when it comes to communicating with the City. It is important that, as part of the HR contribution, prioritisation takes place, and this will require some hard decisions from those in HR. So, a tremendous, award-winning training programme that is the pride of HR may actually be less important to the City than the management of the pension fund; the major recruitment exercise to open a new call centre in Newcastle may be less interesting to the City than the closure of a manufacturing centre (because of the cost reduction possibilities of the latter). HR will not be able to decide on its priorities independently. These will always be part of the overall communication prioritisation, and close alliance with the organisation's business, PR and communication professionals will be necessary.

Step 6 Agree the communications strategy, an outline programme and a budget

The HR elements of the communication to the City will be part of a wider communications strategy and plan. It is important therefore that HR issues are fully represented as part of the plan and not as an afterthought. So the HR professional will need to earn his or her place in the process and provide input accordingly.

Step 7 Involve the operating companies

This is particularly important for the larger organisation that may be handling its communications corporately from the centre. In HR terms this means that a central HR function should keep its subsidiary HR functions involved in the preparation of any communication with the City. It is as bad for an HR employee to read about the organisation's HR plans in the press as for any other employee.

Step 8 Allocate responsibilities

Who is responsible for dealing with the HR input to the City communication? This is important. There are several reasons for allocating responsibility to a single area. First, there is a need to be consistent. This is better achieved by having a single area responsible for co-ordination, and so one of the priorities for those in HR is to decide exactly who this person or persons are. A body of expertise can then be built up to deal with the different demands. Second, a single point of accountability is often a good principle for this type of communication, given the fact that the CEO will probably want direct briefings and will therefore need a clear source of information.

Step 9 Sell the programme internally

It is important that the external City communication is understood by internal stakeholders as well. This can be achieved by those in HR making sure that people issues are included as part of a wider communication strategy and plan.

Step 10 Don't stop planning!

Planning HR communications to the City is not a one-off event.

SOME ACTUAL HR OUTPUTS OF RELEVANCE TO THE CITY

All this is fine, but what are the actual outputs of HR when it comes to interfacing with the City? The following are some of the areas in which HR will have to be proactive.

Annual people report

One of the ways in which the 'people' elements of a company's performance might be articulated is in the production of an annual people report. This would either be an addendum to the annual financial report or as a separate document. The annual people report would include, typically:

- analyses of overall headcount movement for the year, and a comparison with that of previous years

- information on levels of recruitment and turnover
- information on the make-up of the workforce by age, gender and ethnic origin
- information on pay and reward, in totality and by particular groups
- key milestones in change programmes
- new people policies
- information on staff attitudes
- information on training ratios, spend and activity
- benchmarks against industry or top-performing company norms.

The annual people report is something that would provide City analysts with key information useful in supplementing other strategic information. It is also something that can be issued to all staff as a way of keeping them informed about people matters.

Analyst briefings

At results time it is likely that the CEO and key board members will conduct a series of road-shows to City analysts and reporters. Mostly the information will be about the financial make up of the organisation. But more and more they will want to know about such things as executive succession, employment trends within the organisation (productivity for example), and any 'one-off' employment announcements. Those in HR should be prepared for these briefings by providing the CEO and his team with a professionally produced HR input to the overall briefing pack.

The annual general meeting (AGM)

Once the annual performance figures have been announced the annual general meeting will take place. This is in theory available to all shareholders, who will be asked to vote on the acceptance of the financial report, approve senior appointments (including non-executive directors) and raise any specific questions. Trade unions or employee representatives will also want their say and will be likely to raise issues about executive pay, recruitment or redundancy programmes or any strategic moves such as outsourcing. Those in HR will have to ensure that those on the panel for the AGM, usually the board, are prepared to answer any 'people' questions, and they should themselves be available if the chairman wishes to call on them directly (fairly unusual, since the CEO normally fields such questions).

Press releases

Finally, HR are likely to be consulted about any releases to the financial press about company performance as far as it relates to people issues. Knowing what information to provide and in what format is something in which the HR professional will want to be competent. Indeed, it may be that those in HR will relate to the financial press directly in the event of 'special' announcements (the appointment of senior directors, a new retail outlet opening, a factory closing). Developing good presentation and interviewing skills will be important in this respect.

When preparing a press release the following should be included (Rouse and Rouse 2002):

- the name and logo of the organisation
- the date the release was issued
- the main purpose of the release – a summary of the message and relevant supporting information or facts
- notes to editors
- contact details of the author of the release.

Finally, it is essential that the information presented in one communication is the same as that in another. This is a pretty obvious thing to say, but mistakes can happen, perhaps inadvertently as final 'tweaks' are made to the information as it goes public. It's important that an eye is kept on the consistency of the information as it is presented.

CONCLUSION: AREAS OF DEVELOPMENT FOR THE HR PROFESSIONAL

In defining HR's role in the organisation's relationship with the City, I have tried to outline some of the most important areas of involvement. Inevitably this is not comprehensive and will be different in different organisations. One thing is consistent, though, and that is the growing nature of the role. So what should the HR professional do to prepare for this new challenge? The following are a few possible areas of development:

- Understand the organisation's strategy and how it proposes to present this to financial stakeholders. In this way a better HR response will be forthcoming.
- Anticipate the likely 'people' issues that arise out of the organisation's presentation to the City, and make sure there is sufficient data available.
- Keep up-to-date key ratios so that these are not seen as an 'event' on an *ad hoc* basis (headcount and turnover, recruitment and redundancy levels, training investment and so on).
- Develop presentation skills so that in the event of being called on to do a press or PR interview, you, as an HR professional, are fully prepared.

In an increasingly media-aware world, the HR community will have to work hard to make sure that it is fully up to speed on all requirements when relating to the City in all its guises.

10

HR and the Media

I think it would be nice to run a newspaper. Citizen Kane (1941)

The HR profession has definitely got a lot more savvy in its dealings with the media during the 15 or so years I've been writing about personnel and development. Broadly speaking, there have been three distinct phases. During phase one – the 1980s – it was easy to find HR people willing to give a quote on any subject under the sun. Trained as industrial relations fire-fighters, and used to speaking their minds, this breed was a journalist's dream and a PR practitioner's nightmare (until they became extinct). An article in Personnel Management *magazine from that era told the story of the company that opened its annual pay negotiations on the day it announced its latest spectacular profit figures!*

Phase two – most of the 1990s – was a grim time for journalists. After the recession that opened the decade, HR managers seemed scared of the press. Journalists would automatically be referred to the PR department – if we were lucky. This was the era in which a representative from one organisation told me 'We don't talk to the press unless there's something in it for us' (and they weren't the only ones). Never a wise move – the journalist concerned could still be retelling that anecdote five years later…

It's hard to say when phase three began – it sort of crept up on us without any fanfare. Senior HR people started going on media training courses, or role-playing with experienced journalists from newspapers, magazines and broadcasting. They learned a few simple rules, such as:

- *Don't tell lies (you'll be found out).*

- *Don't exaggerate or wing it (see above).*

- *If in doubt about the answer to a question, ask for more time and promise to get back to them.*

- *Keep that promise.*

- *Don't ignore journalists' calls and hope they'll go away – it's better to find out what they want.*

- *Get professional help if you think there's something odd going on.*

Of course, there are still problems; but on the whole it's a far more grown-up world these days.

Steve Crabbe, Editor, People Management

INTRODUCTION

A shiver runs down your spine. The press office has just called. The *Financial Times* want an interview with HR about the reasons for the recent redundancies and the effect they may have on the local community. Could you talk to them? You break into a cold sweat. This follows your interview yesterday with the *Sun* and *Daily Mirror* about the sexual discrimination case that was being heard at Croydon Employment Tribunal. Then, to top it all, Sky News have just asked you to appear on a piece they are running about stress in the workplace.

Then you wake up. Fortunately, *People Management* and *Personnel Today* want to run a friendly piece on the award your organisation has just won for its corporate university. The trials and tribulations of HR and its relationship with the media...

For most people in HR it's a relatively unusual experience to have to deal with the media. But the proliferation of news delivery channels and the hunger for information – especially about people-related matters – means that those in HR are more likely to be fielded to the media. There's nowhere to hide. We now have to face up to the fearsome beast that we know as the British press. But is it really so scary? Surely the press have a key role to play in a free and democratic society. If so, can't we expect to have a fair hearing and have our organisational voice represented in a balanced way?

The answer is yes, most of the time. (But when you hear politicians giving answers that they'd prepared the day before about questions that haven't actually been asked you may wonder!) The reality is that HR people have to have an approach to dealing with the media. If they don't then the media will report as they see – with or without the input of the HR professional. The media don't normally need permission to print – that is the essence of a free press. So HR professionals should try to become conversant with the 'rules'. This chapter discusses some principles about HR's involvement with and presentation to the media. It will not, of course, give an ideal solution for every situation. It will give guidelines to be used in an appropriate way. The chapter also comes with a health warning: press briefings can go wrong as well as right!

WHAT DO WE MEAN BY THE MEDIA, AND WHY SHOULD HR BE CONCERNED?

We all have views about the media. Some of the more critical are unfounded. (I put this in just in case this chapter goes horribly wrong!) Stephen Glover's analysis of the role of the journalist – a key figure in the media – noted that 'We may hate journalists – indeed we rank them, according to some polls, below estate agents and politicians. But hating is not knowing them. How do they work? How is it done? What are the skills involved?' (Glover 1999). This would seem to be a pretty fundamental place to start if we are to learn how we can work with the press and other media in a positive way.

'The media' is a broad description of a diverse group of activities embracing a whole range of different approaches and styles. The common theme that runs through all of them is the intention to communicate news or information. This can be sensationalist ('London Bus Found on Moon'), quirky ('Four Thousand Holes in Blackburn, Lancashire') or merely local ('Man Bites Dog in Norwich'). It can be emotional or objective, topical or historical. But one thing is for sure: news and news interest is pervasive. Maybe it always has been, in one form or another.

There are different views about the media and journalism from within. A N Wilson observed that, in his opinion, journalism was 'more a branch of imaginative literature than it is an exact science. Many newspaper readers make the mistake of hoping that these sketchbooks of the world which we call newspapers will provide a picture of How Things Really Are. But that is an illusion' (Wilson 1999). And in *Ulysses* James Joyce – under the headline *How a Great Daily Organ Is Turned Out* – has his central character ponder that 'It's the ads and side features sell a weekly not the stale news in the official gazette.'

But there are more circumspect views. John Pilger, for example, has described journalism as an honourable tradition, combating the notion of a 'free' press undermined by a monopoly that serves up 'distortion, non-news, violence and soap suds, anti-journalism' (Pilger 1986). Emma Daly, referring to her experiences 'in the front line', wrote 'You don't have to visit a war zone to find compelling stories and to learn about the human spirit, but it helps' (Daly 1999).

With the advent of electronic communication there has also been a shift in the definition of the media – the replacement of 'hot' media with 'cool' media. Marshall McLuhan has described this as follows:

> *Speech is a cool medium of low definition, because so little is given and so much has to be filled in by the listener. On the other hand, hot media do not leave so much to be filled in or completed by the audience. Hot media are therefore low in participation, and cool media are high in participation or completion by the audience.* Stevenson 2002

Telephony and the Web might be described as cool media. The use of the Web by the media, in our definition, has therefore added a new dimension to the area as more and more media such as newspapers or TV offer an online alternative.

What we have here in Britain are of course media rich in diversity, tapping into the gossip about celebs on the one hand but on the other presenting some of the best 'serious' journalism in the world. This is the context within which the HR professional can find him- or herself when dealing with the human interest stories that concern the employees of the organisation.

A RICH SOURCE OF INFORMATION

To add to this richness, the media are not a single entity. It is not the newspaper or the TV that makes up our definition of the media. These are just two of the 'channels' by which information is communicated to the public domain. Amongst the things we may put into the category of media are:

- television
- radio
- newspapers
- magazines
- specialist journals

- web-based publications
- news sheets.

It is possible that any one of these would want information and opinion on people matters that are in the province of HR. Some examples of this from a cursory examination on a single day are:

- a comment on the management and leadership style of Sven-Göran Eriksson after England's performance in the World Cup of 2002
- an item in the Sundays about Gordon Brown's plan to change pension arrangements
- a newspaper article about career change involving a former 'Bond Girl' who became a property dealer
- an article about the work–life balance in the House of Commons
- scores of Web-based human interest news stories.

These are people matters that matter to people. In more and more of this type of article the views of the 'people expert' are being called for. They include academics who have specialised in such matters as stress or training, legal experts, government watchers, and of course HR professionals. The views are given by experts on the technicalities of the subject, then converted to written or spoken articles by expert journalists. These articles get published in the media. The question we face as HR professionals is how far we want to go in contributing to them. In the past this has been a rare or occasional question. Increasingly, though, it is becoming more commonplace. So what should we look for when dealing with the media?

WHAT ISSUES ARE LIKELY TO COME UP IN THE MEDIA?

In the typical day (if such a thing exists) of the HR professional it would be rare to have many issues that would be considered newsworthy. However, there is an increasing interest in people matters, whether or not they make the local magistrates court or employment tribunal or (for that matter) influence the City pages. It is a fact of life for HR therefore that keeping a finger on the pulse for possible media interest is an essential activity. Here are some of the issues that may arise:

- At the highest level it is almost certain that the annual reporting season will bring with it its stock of people issues, and these must be anticipated. It's likely that the press office or PR firm will want a response from HR on them. People implications of press statements to the City – recruitment or redundancy; the appointment or sacking of a chief executive or director; international expansion and its people implications; or the HR outcomes of merger and acquisition. A recent example was in the *Times* Business section of 30 November 2002. In response to a decision by Safeway to scrap their Christmas bonus, the HR director was quoted extensively.
- At the middle level an employment tribunal has a chance of appearing in the local press – possibly the national press if it's of sufficient news value (or if it's a slow news day). There may also be people implications of business decisions affecting the

community, local or otherwise, such as factory or office closures, or the opening of a new retailing outlet.

- At a local level anything from charitable presentations to driving bans can demand a press response. Nowadays there may be employment tribunals, articles and reports about disaffected employees, whistle-blowing or awards – from Investors in People at one end of the scale to individual awards at the other (the Honours list, for example).

It is necessary for HR to be able to put all these news items in context and to understand the needs of the journalists who have to prepare the copy and provide information in a way that represents the whole picture. It is not advisable to attempt the cover-up, the false picture or the 'clever' manipulation of the media. Most probably these will come unstuck, with disastrous consequences.

HOW MIGHT HR BEST DEAL WITH THE MEDIA?

'Fortress HR' is not going to satisfy media looking for and expecting organisations to give them information. As one commentator has noted, 'News knows no boundaries', and this applies as much to people issues dealt with by HR professionals as any other. Dealing with the media, then, is an important aspect of the HR professional's role. So what might be done? Are there any guiding principles that we might adopt?

The first thing to note is that there will be occasions when there is a difference between what you want to publicise and what the particular journal you're talking to wants the world to know. If PR is desired, then 'the only way to achieve media coverage is to give the media what it wants, how and when it wants it' (Jefkins 1987). This might be fine for some aspects of media coverage by the HR professional – mainly successes or straight information transmission – but how can this be reconciled with the times when we definitely don't want media coverage? My view is that it can't, and this is the dilemma facing most of us who work in HR – hence the deafening silence from most HR professionals when it comes to the media. In the past, this has been a very wise policy. But for all the reasons outlined in earlier chapters – the talent war, the need to raise the profile of the organisation as a responsible employer and so on – this is less tenable as an HR position. You can't court publicity as a great place to work to an external audience and then expect to be selective about what gets published. Neither can you stonewall and hope that the media will go away. If there is a story, it will get published, whether the HR professional comments or not. So are there things that can be done to mitigate the downside of media relations?

It's generally regarded that there are four key things to bear in mind when dealing with journalists and the media (Graham 1995). These are critical in determining the HR response and position and can be summarised as:

- a fast reaction to enquiries
- an open and honest media relations policy
- a willingness to deal with unfavourable news
- comprehensible information.

What things can the HR professional and indeed HR department do to ensure they are in a position to respond to these requirements?

Fast reaction to enquiries

In the first instance it is worth considering having a member of the HR team who can act as single point of interface to either the press office or the PR company who handle press relations. The role of this person will be twofold. First, he or she will provide a rapid reaction to the enquiry. This may be the actual answer or a holding statement until an answer can be obtained. If the latter, then there should be a guarantee that a response will be given within an agreed time. The second role is to act as expert guide to who should field the response. If it's a trade union matter, then this will normally be the employee relations professional. If it's about pay, then the reward professional, and so on. Of course it is equally likely that the senior managers of the organisation will want to respond with a line manager statement. If this is the case, then those in HR will act as advisers and prepare the statement.

Open and honest media relations policy

The two questions in response to this are, 'Do we have a media relations policy for HR?' and 'Why have one in the first place?' The answer to both is because if those in the media rumble the fact that the organisation's spokesperson has been less than honest or has tried to cover up any issue, tried to be clever, or tried to pull the wool over their eyes, then they will turn savage. And savage media in an open, democratic society can be really savage. The rule is: don't mislead the media! If something is confidential, such as an acquisition, don't mislead. Say it is not possible to comment on this subject or say 'Yes, the company is looking for international partners.' It is a risky strategy to deny such a move on one day and then announce the deal the next.

Some organisations cultivate media relationships that they regard as precious. 'Cultivating' means building up a position of trust with journalists so that when it really is too difficult, they will respect that. Likewise when there is a statement it will be sufficiently open, have sufficient detail and be interesting. This is the *quid pro quo*, although of course it isn't as straightforward as that.

From an HR perspective, it is worth considering what this position of openness and honesty means. Of course, respect for the privacy of an individual employee is paramount. So any communication that is open can only be so if it has taken account of the wishes of the individual.

A policy on dealing with the media from an HR perspective is included at Figure 19 and displays the following features:

1   *A single point of entry into the organisation.* This can mean that all media enquiries are directed to the press office or the public relations company used by the organisation. A statement that no independent response to the media is given before directing to or consulting with the specialist press area is a wise one. This allows a co-ordination of all press responses to ensure consistency

2   *A process for a rapid, professional response providing the necessary information.* In particular the need here is to join up the HR response to the overall organisation

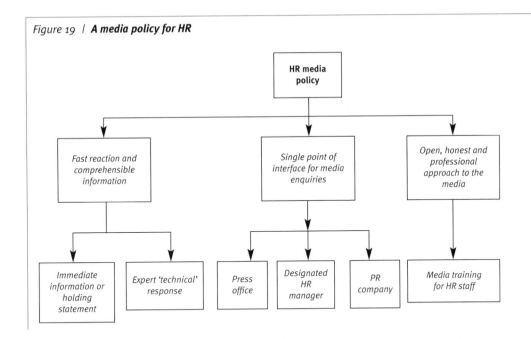

Figure 19 / **A media policy for HR**

position and then make sure that all aspects of HR are covered. An example may be in response to a question about outsourcing. Let's say that the organisation is considering outsourcing its technology processing to India – a not uncommon strategic option. The press get wind of this and want to know what the organisation's position really is. There will be strategic questions about positioning within the overall approach to technology, questions about cost and reliability and, most importantly to the HR professional, questions about job losses in the home territory, cultural fit and employee relations. The HR action is therefore twofold:

– Make sure that the HR response is in line with the business strategy.

– Make sure that all the HR bases are covered – that the decision is presented within the context of the people strategy, has been clearly communicated to employees and that union briefings have taken place.

Furthermore, the internal employee briefings will have to have taken place before the announcement hits the Sunday headlines. There is nothing more difficult to deal with than a pre-emptive press story before the news has been communicated internally. It does happen, of course, but the more this can be anticipated, the better the chance of dealing with the people issues.

3 *An HR professional fully conversant with the particular skills and training for giving a media response.* The importance of this point cannot be overstated. It's not that the media are out to deceive; it's just that they will be expecting a response that allows them to give an interesting and informative story. To do so might require an approach that is more than the mere presentation of statistics. They will be looking for a hook

that is going to attract their readers. If HR professionals are going to be involved in this process, they will have to understand how to convey this information. A policy on training for the media is therefore a necessary outcome of HR's greater involvement.

So this provides at least the basis for a policy on media communication from an HR perspective.

Willingness to deal with unfavourable news

It's an unfortunate part of the HR professional's role that bad news is sometimes a consequence of the people responsibility. Those in HR have to deal with the horrible things that sometimes result from a change of strategy. Dealing with redundancy – one of the most distressing things that can happen to an employee – often falls within the role specification of HR. Counselling for stress caused by organisational changes of one sort or another is a further part of the bad news part of the job. But it does go with the patch, and HR people deal with this as a matter of course and in a professional manner. But what about when bad or unfavourable news goes public? What things fall into this category, and what is the process for HR to deal with such an item?

Unfavourable news can come from a variety of sources:

- *Nationally or organisation-wide.* Inevitably the decision to close part of the operation will hit the press if it involves mass redundancy or job loss. Motorola, Ford, Consignia and BT are amongst the household names that in recent times have had to break news to the public of job losses or significant restructuring. It is never easy and there is no way to interpret such news as anything but bad. The days of seeing this type of thing as an opportunity have been confined to the dustbin of employment history. So how should it be managed? Here are a few things that should always be followed when breaking news of this type. It should be:

  - factual

  - sensitive

  - objective.

  Trying to spin this type of stuff will backfire!

- *Regionally or locally.* This can refer to local job losses or a specific employment tribunal case. If so, then the local HR support will have to deal with it. The policy outlined above will make sure that at least such things will be on the radar. However, this type of unfavourable news can be a nightmare. The most common theme is the employment tribunal that gets national coverage, either because of a slow news day or the scale of the award or because the issue is of national interest. The problem is caused by the speed at which the local becomes national. Often there is no warning unless the media ask for comment. A story of the case can be put on the wires, picked up overnight and published before a reasonable response can be given.

Again there are a few things that can be done to mitigate the adverse reaction to such news:

- Align the HR response with the business response. This means making sure that the HR response is seen in context and not as a single, unrelated event.

- Don't try to hide the bad news or, worse, bury it – that can have catastrophic consequences. If it's bad, it's bad. The best thing to do is to be honest.

- Explain any HR activities that are being undertaken to ease the pain associated with the bad news. For example, is redeployment being offered to those whose jobs are going? Is retraining being offered?

Bad news does happen, it does have people consequences, the facts should be given and the mitigating factors should be explained. The best that can be expected from this is a less unfavourable response, so don't expect brownie points. But do be proactive and honest.

Comprehensible information

One of the most common and yet easily averted problems associated with HR media communications is incomprehensibility. Instead of 'yes' or 'no' or even, God forbid, 'don't know' we see attempts at refraction. When simple facts and statements are called for we see opacity instead of clarity – and all this based on either a wish to conceal or a lack of understanding of what is required. It is a bugbear of the journalist and it is something that needs to be addressed if a good media strategy is to be achieved.

George Orwell once lambasted certain types of writing characterised by 'long passages which are almost completely lacking in meaning', and he even went so far as to refer to them as 'a catalogue of swindles and perversions' – in a literary sense, of course (Orwell (1942) 1972). We in HR have to ensure that we don't fall into the trap of incomprehensibility in either our written or spoken communication with the media, that we don't, as *Private Eye* might once have said, get ourselves into an 'incomprehensibility situation' situation.

What things can be used therefore to ensure that the things we say and do in our communication with the media can be understood? There are a few fairly straightforward pointers in this direction:

- Make sure that we don't lapse into HR technical-speak, that the things we present are done so in clear language. Remember, to almost everyone but HR and actuaries, AESOP wrote fables.

- Have a clear message. If the message to be communicated is 'This year's pay pot is 3 per cent' then why say 'Owing to a downturn in the economy post September 11 and a polarisation in the insurance market, it has been necessary to revise this year's annual pay award downwards.' The support information can come later.

- Present the message clearly – which is not the same as the above point. This means being confident in the approach, providing the environment in which the message can be heard and using the most appropriate way to deliver it.

- Provide enough information to support the point being made, but not so much that the point gets lost in complex detail.

- Give room for questions of clarification.

These few simple points are not the only ways that comprehensibility can be achieved. They are intended merely to give a direction.

What we have in the above are a few simple methods for ensuring that the HR professional is able to deal with the media on issues of people matters that get into the public domain. What can the HR professional undertake to enhance this position?

WHAT PREPARATION OR TRAINING CAN BE UNDERTAKEN?

Given the necessity to get HR up to speed in their dealings with the media on issues of people communication, preparation can be made to enhance the competence of the HR professional:

- *Training in media communication.* There are several training packages that can be undertaken by the HR professional. These include one-on-one, tailored approaches – there are several very good organisations that can deliver these, and the programmes themselves are often coupled with interview work with practising TV or newspaper journalists.

- *Self-development* – identifying the key aspects associated with good communication and applying them in practice.

- *Dialogue with the press office or the public relations organisation* – asking them what they expect and gaining insights into the needs of journalists.

Whichever way is chosen, it is essential the HR professional takes an interest in the media communication policy and strategy of the organisation and develops an HR equivalent accordingly.

CONCLUSION

Dealing with the media is something that HR professionals will have to do more and more. The media are a diverse set of people with a diverse set of demands. A common theme, though, is the demand for timely, comprehensible information. HR professionals need to acknowledge this if they are to support the organisation's public face and protect its private one. Understanding the principles of media management and having sufficient competence to deal with all but the most complex issues are a basic requirement of today's HR professional.

Part 4
Internal communication

11

Leading employee communication – an HR responsibility

People here are funny. They work so hard at living they forget how to live. Mr Deeds
Goes to Town (1936)

INTRODUCTION

When Marks and Spencer (M&S) put in place their 'planned recovery', HR was seen as a key enabler. Part of the process was 'recognising the need to involve and include staff . . . resulting in the formation of business involvement groups' (Whittington, Mayer and Smith 2002). This was recognition of the fact that employee engagement does not happen without effective employee communication. To achieve the commitment of the employees to the organisation's strategic direction therefore requires an outstanding communication programme. Those in HR have a key role to play in this. The main reason is that we have been entrusted with providing many of the tools and techniques that facilitate employee engagement: learning, training and development; performance management; participation processes; and, now, effective employee communication. After all, we are the professionals responsible for all aspects of human development. But it's not easy.

Amongst the many challenges facing the chief executive officer (CEO) is the need to gain the commitment of employees to the strategy, policy and principles of the organisation. A recent report by Booz, Allen and Hamilton, an advisory firm, described this challenge as 'endemic' (*Financial Times* 3 December 2002). Indeed, a characteristic of great leadership, as outlined by Deepak Chopra, is the ability to empower the team by walking the talk, declaring and living up to values, and asking for feedback (Chopra 2002). Recognising these factors and being able to implement them organisation-wide seem to be critical to the success of the leader of the organisation. This is a recurring theme, and one that will continue to be so with the advent of such initiatives as the EU Information and Consultation Directive due to come into force in the next three years. Whereas a few years ago 'meeting the challenge of the restless, demanding employee is a major assignment of present-day industrial relations' (Hefty 1991), the twenty-first century has seen this challenge reach even higher levels of difficulty.

Yet we have to get this sorted out. Gaining employee commitment is regarded as an essential prerequisite to achieving the organisation's objectives. Commitment can be as broad as 'the overall strategy of the organisation' or as narrow as 'improve customer service'. One element in gaining this commitment is to make sure that there is an efficient, all-embracing and effective communication process, something that continues to tax even the most innovative executive.

Unfortunately these laudable objectives don't seem to have delivered much; the track record is poor. A recent *Harvard Business Review* article noted that 'most value statements are bland, toothless, or just plain dishonest ... empty value statements create cynical and dispirited employees, alienate customers and undermine managerial credibility' (Lencioni 2002). Recent research showed that 'the employees' ability to recall the company's official values was generally poor' (Murphy and Mackenzie Davey 2002), in part due to ineffective communication. If communication with employees is the critical success factor, then everything must be done to spread the message. We also know that 'the colour of the vans and the fact that everyone wears a name badge doesn't impress anyone without action to back it up. It's the experience that matters, not the gloss' (Morris 2000). It's likely that there'll be three questions associated with the process:

- Why are we communicating with the employees?
- What do we want to communicate?
- How are we going to do so?

The following chapter is intended to answer these questions.

WHY – THE CHANGING PATTERNS OF EMPLOYEE INVOLVEMENT AND COMMUNICATION

It may sound a bit trite but effective employee communication and its conversion into understanding of, agreement on and the delivery of personal objectives that fit in with wider business objectives is really key to how well the organisation will do. In the private sector, communicating the objectives of the organisation, how a business unit or department fits in, where an employee can make the most contribution and, most importantly, where progress is being made (or not) is tantamount to defining success. Without these factors the employee is operating in an information vacuum, not knowing what is expected or what has been achieved. In the public sector the same points apply, and it's important that clarity of purpose for the department and the individual is sought, communicated, understood and reciprocated. We saw in Chapter 3 that the nature of work in the modern organisation had accentuated the need to have a better approach to employee communication. The effect would be the desire of all organisations – employee engagement.

So what are the main benefits of a comprehensive employee communication programme?

- First and foremost, employees who know what's going on in the organisation and what's expected of them are more likely to feel motivated towards the achievement of the organisation's objectives. The Sears work (Rucci, Kirn and Quinn 1998) demonstrated the link between employee satisfaction and customer satisfaction.

Improve the former and the latter will also improve. An important part of this, as shown by attitude surveys the world over, is the feeling of 'a great place to work'. In a great place to work employees are informed. And this means communication that gets through. There has been a good deal of emphasis on this particular issue. Recent reports have outlined worldwide programmes to deal with this by such organisations as Thyssen Krupp, the German engineering firm, BP and General Electric (*Financial Times* 3 December 2002).

- So it would seem essential that in order to put their own role in context, employees know the strategic direction of the organisation. Otherwise everyone will be working in a narrow silo, unaware of their wider contribution. There is unlikely to be engagement with the organisation in this case. When B-Sky-B wanted to implement their CRM vision, it was considered essential that their employees spoke 'with one voice'. The effective communication strategy articulated at the 2002 Harrogate Conference involved top-down, bottom-up and horizontal communication through a variety of channels (McCoy 2002). When Cable and Wireless wanted to put in their new HRIS, a communication and engagement strategy was considered vital to success (Pickard 2002).

- If employees are made aware of how their own role fits in with that of their colleagues in pursuit of the objectives, then a more joined-up approach will be achieved. This is an important aspect, in that any one employee, manager or director will be aware of how his or her actions either add to or detract from the performance of colleagues in other areas.

- Effective communication will contribute to the delivery of better customer service as it ties into the concept of a seamless organisation.

- Communicating effectively with employees is necessary in the objective-setting process.

- Two-way communication allows ideas and contributions from employees to come through.

So here are some important reasons for improving employee communication. But what type of information should be communicated?

WHAT INFORMATION SHOULD WE COMMUNICATE TO EMPLOYEES?

There are two sides to the coin of employee communication. The first is that on which most organisations will focus, ie 'What does the organisation want the employees to know?' But a key question in employee communication is 'What do *employees* want to know?' Getting both right will require some effort.

What does the organisation want employees to know?

This question is the most researched. At the highest level it's assumed that an organisation would want its employees to obey the law and act ethically in their dealings with customers. It's further assumed that the organisation would want to make sure that employees understood the opportunities available to them, and that the needs of a diverse population were met (Guirdham 1999). The HR community has a big part to play in preparing the information that satisfies these requirements through:

- the principles of employment – eg guidelines about how the organisation expects its employees to behave towards each other (performance management coaching at one end of the spectrum, policies to deal with bullying and harassment at the other)

- the implications of employment law and how these should be applied (recruitment, referencing, terms and conditions of service and so on)

- customer service standards, to be produced by those responsible for marketing – but the training to achieve these standards is probably the duty of HR, so there is a likely requirement to issue performance standards for customer service as part of the role specification, and training standards as part of the training plan

- the publication of job vacancies

- the publication of diversity standards and policies.

Each of these will need more attention to communication than may have been the case in the recent past. Why is that? Well, first, the information is likely to be in competition with other types of information; second, there is probably more 'people information' than before; and third, the communication will have to be in the format that employees are used to and respect in the modern communication environment.

When it comes down to the business of management, it is generally concluded that a manager's responsibility will be to inform the employee about 'the work unit mission: progress; individual job responsibility: standards; individual performance feedback; individuals' needs and concerns; information suggestions, proposals upward; and the work unit's place in the company' (D'Aprix 1982). These are very much the managerial perspective of what employees need to know. This view is reinforced by the following (after Bland 1980):

Progress	Product sales, market share, trading position, financial results
Profitability	Income and distribution of income, net company profit
Plans and policies	Health and safety, job evaluation, policies on gender, race and disability
People	Appointments, promotions, resignations, turnover, training.

This type of approach is what will be present in most organisations. But there is another side to the story: the views of the employees!

What do employees say they want to know?

Organisations continue to grapple with the challenge of effective communication as a part of an engagement process deemed necessary for success. But research into this area has shown that organisations have a good way to go before they can win hearts and minds. The Gallup Organisation survey results presented in 2001 (Buckingham and Wilde 2001) showed how much of a challenge this was.

These results come at a time when the engagement of employees at work is regarded as a key differentiator for success. The heat is bound to be on therefore to improve this situation, to make sure that employees are fully committed and that competitive advantage can follow. Indeed, corporate change will not be successful without the effectiveness of the communication, which is a matter not only of the transference of information but also of the instilling of a trusting relationship. Even 20 years ago it was considered essential that an organisation should 'convey and emphasize trust in all matters (and especially communication) related to change' (Deal and Kennedy 1982). We have to ask why the results of this have not been very good.

So when we come to decide on the question of what employees really want to know, here's a great idea: *why don't you ask them?* Surely the essential starting point for this engagement process is to understand the communication needs of the employees as well as those of the organisation as an employer. One without the other will give a distorted view. We should therefore deliver solutions that satisfy the needs of all stakeholders where possible. It is a key role of the HR professional to pull together the diverse strands of data about employee attitudes and opinions and convert these into rich sources of information from which we can deliver coherent communication based on what employees want to know.

There is often an unintended divergence of views between the two positions of employer and employee perceptions. Sometimes senior managers will be interested in p/e ratios, whilst employees want to know why the share price has gone up or down. There may be a high-level focus on talent, succession and senior management development, whilst the employees want to know how they are going to be trained a) to do their current job and b) to do their next job. These are the same subjects from a different perspective. What is really needed is for HR to act as the filter through which the many issues pass about what employees want to know and then to convert these into meaningful communication. To do so will require HR to be proactive in all aspects of employee communication.

There are tools and techniques by which a view can be gained of employee attitudes and information needs. Some of these are:

- staff attitude surveys
- communication audits
- focus groups
- team meetings with feedback capture
- bulletin boards
- helplines
- 'frequently asked question' analyses (from such things as Web-based HR policy manuals).

The key is to make sure that there is an understanding that this information is important and that there is a way of converting the data into meaningful information that can be used by an HR professional in setting up communication strategies and plans for employees. Without this process communication is a one-way affair – ie it isn't communication at all.

So it is clear that there may be two perspectives on employee communication: what the employer thinks the employee wants to know, and what the employee actually wants to know. Effective employee communication is about satisfying both needs.

HOW – TYPES OF EMPLOYEE COMMUNICATION

The importance of employee communications is not new. The recognition that 'we have to take the people along with us' is something of which all good managers are aware. The way we actually achieve this desirable objective has also been around for a good while. There have been great strides made through technology having a greater part to play in communication, and recent developments in intranets and the Internet have added an even more attractive dimension. You would think, wouldn't you, that the communication process is easier. But just when we have solved the issue of rapid global communications through technology, we read that it is now too impersonal. Getting employee communication right is difficult.

Communicating with employees is not just a nice way of demonstrating that the senior management of the organisation are human after all. Nor is it merely a way of 'finding out what employees think'. So many organisational processes depend on the effectiveness of communication. The success of performance management systems, for example, would not be possible without good communication. To achieve good performance management, mission statements are needed that reinforce corporate messages, and business plans have to be agreed that clarify objectives (Marchington and Wilkinson 1998). In both cases an appropriate means of two-way communication is necessary. When communicating with disabled employees this is a particularly important point. Not only do we have to recognise the requirements of the Disability Discrimination Act, but we shall also fail to maximise the potential of an extremely valuable sector of the workforce unless we make provisions to communicate effectively.

So what types of employee communication exist?

Guest and Conway's (2002) recent research has shown a variety of methods that have been used to communicate 'the organisation's promises and commitments to employees'. These included:

- *job communication*
  - individual objectives and targets
  - team targets
  - performance appraisal
  - informal day-to-day interaction
  - briefing by line management
  - training and development

- *recruitment communication*
  - job descriptions
  - induction and initial training
  - the recruitment process
  - the staff handbook/manual
- *top-down communication*
  - mission statements
  - annual company meetings with staff.

This list reflects the diversity of the way in which employee communication takes place. More specific methods are as follows.

Downward communication

It's easy to disparage downward communication. The fact that it is a one-way street means that there is little or no opportunity for adaptation or contextualising. Nonetheless it remains a common form of information transmission.

Leopold (2002) has noted that with downward communication, the principle objective is 'for managers to inform and educate employees directly so that they accept management plans. A variety of techniques is available that vary in their degree of formality/informality, in their regularity and in whether they rely on oral or written communication, and whether they are face to face or direct.' At its most basic, then, employee communication is simply a vertical transference from the top to the bottom of the organisation.

Downward communication has many advantages, some of which are:

- It's a quick way of getting important information out.
- If it's simple, it's an effective way of achieving a consistent message – there's less debate or interpretation.
- It can add personality to the senior management team if delivered effectively.

So it's not always wrong just to have downward communication. The context for this, though, has to be right.

Upward communication

The counterpart to downward communication is, of course, upward communication. This is an area that in most organisations is at best mediocre and at worst non-existent. And yet we saw in earlier chapters that communication doesn't exist without a two-way flow of information. Upward communication can (Bevan and Bailey 1991):

- allow employees to contribute information and ideas
- keep management in touch with concerns, issues and questions
- contribute to the development of a shared understanding of organisational goals.

With the advent of technology it should be easier to provide the infrastructure for upward communication. After all, it is good Investor in People (IiP) practice to provide for this activity.

The CEO's website is one such method that has been used successfully (rumour has it that Bill Gates receives scores of e-mails directly from his Microsoft® employees). It appears to be critical to success.

Employee voice

Another way is to embrace the idea of employee voice – which is gaining in importance and credibility. It is part of a whole new approach to partnership. With trade unions this is seen as a move towards a more trusting relationship:

> *At its basis, partnership means giving managers and trade union representatives proper*
> *rights and responsibilities by encouraging a more open and honest approach in exchanges.*
> *No surprises, as opposed to a hidden agenda. Meaningful debate, rather than game-playing.*
> Mead 2002

It is an important concept, essential to the process of effective employee communication.

An increasing body of research (Marchington 2001) is building up around the whole question of employee voice, which means:

- two-way communications/exchange of views
- upward problem-solving – by project teams and attitude surveys
- collective representation – partnership schemes and joint consultation
- employee engagement
- having a say about issues.

We saw in an earlier chapter that there was a real need to communicate effectively with employees. The attitudinal, social and economic shift from industrial democracy to employee involvement has brought with it an emphasis on the individual as opposed to a collective. This is complex. Employee involvement is 'championed by management, often without any great pressure from employees or trade unions and is directed at securing greater employee commitment to, and identification with, the employing organisation' (Marchington and Wilkinson 1998). Furthermore, attitude surveys suggest that employees are 'opposed to a style of leadership which merely informs them about decisions after the event, and appear to favour something in between a "sells" style and a consultative approach' (Marchington 1995). On the upside:

> *Employee involvement in decision-making has been seen as of major importance both with*
> *respect to the quality of life of employees themselves and with respect to managerial objectives of*
> *high levels of commitment and productivity ... those workers who have a greater say in decisions*
> *concerning their jobs are, other things being equal, more likely to be enthusiastic, contented and*
> *satisfied with their work.* Gallie, Felstead and Green 2002

Internal corporate marketing

A variation on the themes of downward and upward communication is 'internal corporate marketing'. We've seen that the communication challenge is to engage employees by providing information that satisfies their needs whilst enabling the organisational strategy. One of the possible solutions is to use the processes of internal corporate marketing: 'in order to entice people to do anything that needs some form of persuasion, it is necessary to find what creates or reinforces the need for them to want to act in a positive and motivated way' (Thomson 1990).

It has been recognised that communication is only a part of the need to engage employees, and that the overall process is one of winning hearts and minds as well as addressing ears and eyes. One way forward is to take a holistic view, ie embrace the wider view of communication as targeting an audience by means of appropriate channels along with appropriate content. There have been attempts to do this: team briefings, quality circles and cascade communications have each been incorporated into organisational communication processes. A further concept is 'internal corporate marketing', a new form of internal communications. It is an attempt to shift communications up a gear.

The idea is to converge marketing and HRM in a complementary way. Such approaches have had some effect, although not universally (and not for want of trying). It's clear there is still some way to go. The thing that has really forced the issue now is the significant social and cultural shift in the organisational context.

Employee engagement

Of course, communication with the modern workforce requires much more than the straightforward passing-on of information. Many organisations have recognised that *engagement* (as opposed to communication) is required – a hearts-and-minds campaign, especially with a media-aware and -influenced working population. What does this mean exactly? Well, for a start, more and more creative methods for getting over the message. Examples of this are:

- business TV, ie media-produced and -directed internal TV programmes about a particular aspect of business change
- the so-called 'stage show' – the use of celebrities to pass on information about change. When Lloyds TSB launched its new brand in 1998, Carol Vorderman was the host to a 2,000-employee spectacular at the NEC in Birmingham. Later, when the company integrated Scottish Widows into the group, Jonathan Ross hosted an event for insurance employees at the BBC studios.

But unless there is some structure to reinforce this, the message may well be lost. So let's take the view earlier that four channels can be used and that the communication has to be adapted accordingly. The four channels identified were face to face, telephony, the Web and mail.

HOW – THE CHANNELS OF EMPLOYEE COMMUNICATION

Communicating with employees needs to take account of all these channels. What specifically can we use in each?

Face to face

There's nothing like walking the talk to communicate a message effectively. Such a method 'enables immediate upward feedback' (Scholes 1999) and is a good opportunity to boost the credibility of the message by its personal approach. Indeed, there are those who would advocate that 'all channels of communication should attempt to achieve the condition of face to face' because 'most mistakes of business communication, both internal and external, occur when the target audience has no face ... you don't communicate with targets' (Bernstein 1984). Face-to-face communication quite literally presents this face!

Face-to-face communication can be achieved through a variety of methods:

- one-on-one communication
- team meetings
- back-to-the-shop-floor programmes.

Most organisations have their own versions of face-to-face communication. For many employers and employees it is the preferred method. Of course, given the complexity of the contemporary organisation that may have many sites, 24/7 working, project-based organisation structures and unrelenting change, the face-to-face method is often combined with others. Technology allows a multichannel approach.

Telephony

Providing information over the phone is no longer an unusual practice. Many HR departments now have HR call centres or telephony-based services that are a valuable addition to the communication armoury – if used appropriately. Organisations like IBM and Standard Chartered have all used telephony via HR call centres or shared-services centres as part of their HR process.

The dos and don'ts of employee communication via telephony are as follows:

- Be very clear and unequivocal in presenting the message – there's little opportunity for interpretation over the phone, nor can the person be engaged as with face to face.
- Be consistent in the communication – ensure that a scripted communication is available that is the same for all of those delivering the message.
- Use clear instructions to make it easy for the employee to access the telephony communication channel.

The use of telephony in HR is increasing in a wide range of subject areas and can be effective if key principles are applied.

The Web and mail

I've combined these sections because some employee communications can be interchanged between the two. The Internet has revolutionised communication in society. It can also be a powerful organisational communication tool. An equally powerful variant is the internal corporate Internet known as the intranet. This is a safe and protected communication channel that can be harnessed by HR in the challenge of employee communication. But let's also remember that physical mail as opposed to e-mail or websites continues to be a common form of communication.

The use of the Web to communicate to employees has been referred to as *B2E management*. The primary drivers for using this type of communication are employee self-service and 'mass customisation' (Hansen and Deimler 2001). The types of communication envisaged by B2E management to employees are:

- online benefits, administration and healthcare information
- online training
- online career development.

If we go back to our earlier discussion of what employees want to know from an organisational communication, we can see that B2E is a powerful addition to the communication channels of the HR professional.

E-mail and the Web in particular are two of the most powerful recent developments in corporate communication and have been harnessed by HR in the form of employee communication. Their strengths lie in the accessibility and speed of the Web. A communication that might once have taken days to distribute throughout the organisation can be done very quickly indeed. (I was going to write instantaneously, but the Web is very slow tonight!) The disadvantages are of course the impersonality of communication through the Web. Therefore it should never replace other techniques but be part of a multichannel approach.

Internal corporate magazine

The corporate magazine (a rather grand-sounding description of a wide variety of staff journals) is a good source of employee communication. The magazine is a growing aspect of social life and 'despite the tabloids, self-created and high-profile publishers know that the real growth in the British reading market over the past ten years across all social groupings has actually been in magazines'. The staff magazine is 'less about new information, more about people and issues "in the news" ... seen as a mix of increased understanding, behind-the-scenes information/education and entertainment' (Scholes 1999).

The company magazine can include:

- information about individual employees – successes in the organisation or in their non-company achievements
- popular descriptions of business strategies or projects – 'popular' is not a pejorative word here but one that recognises that the jargon and acronyms so often used in business need translation for most people outside the immediate sphere of the project in question
- people policies and practices
- business information – profit, sales turnover and so on:
  - information on pay and reward – in totality and by particular groups

- key milestones in change programmes
- information on staff attitudes
- information on training ratios, spend and activity
- benchmarks against industry or top-performing company norms.

Now, we all have an opinion about the magazine as either a wasted propaganda tool disbelieved by the employees or as a valuable and well-loved addition to the communication tools of the organisation. It can certainly be the latter if care is taken to position it as part of a wider employee communication channel mix.

So various channels can be used to deliver employee communication, and developing a channel mix is a key part of the communication process.

HOW – A CASE STUDY

Applying the principles of employee communication: the annual people report

Here we look at a specific example of an employee communication and show how it can be developed and communicated using both the Web and mail. Let's take the annual people report as an example.

We saw in an earlier chapter that the preparation of an annual people report was of use to the City. However, its main role is in presenting the overall 'people' performance to the employees of the organisation. The preparation of the annual people report should be the responsibility of those in HR.

The following is a suggested format for such a communication. It should of course be adapted to the specific context of an organisation and is therefore only a template.

Statement from chief executive
This might take the form of a 'review of employment', starting with the CEO's overall statement of the importance of people and the specific elements of the organisation's success that are most dependent on employee engagement – eg customer service.

Recruitment and overall manpower performance
The first specific subject area would be an overview of the organisation's 'headcount' performance. This will include how many employees work in the organisation, where they work and in what type of jobs. Turnover, recruitment and redeployment should also be included.

Pay and reward
This section will include information on basic salary, the total pay bill, pay increases and any profit-sharing. It will also refer to bonus payments, share option plans and pensions.

Learning, training and development
The commitment of the organisation to provide learning, training and develop-

ment opportunities is something in which employees will be particularly interested. Often the totality of training provision is not communicated. The annual people report is a perfect opportunity to do so.

Occupational health

If the organisation provides schemes that support an individual's health and well-being whilst at work then this might be included in the report. Such factors as healthcare provision, sports and social facilities and activities, sickness and absence support and so on could be outlined.

Commitment to national initiatives

An obvious inclusion here would be any work to secure IiP recognition. The progress of the organisation could be reported. National Quality Awards, training initiatives (such as National Learning at Work Day) or other well-publicised activities are also worthy of mention.

General employment communication

The annual people report is an excellent opportunity to wrap all the people initiatives for the year into a single publication. Any policy changes such as flexible working or equal pay are of interest to all employees and should be included.

The annual people report is then an opportunity for the organisation to let its employees know of the investment that has taken place during the year in a range of people matters. Having prepared it, you then have to think about how to distribute the end product. Several ways are available:

Through the Web

This is a very cost-effective way of communicating the annual people report to employees, particularly if they are on dispersed sites. Of course, those in HR will have to ensure that people have access to the Web – whether through the corporate intranet site (if such a thing exists) or through the Internet. In one example of a 'Review of Employment' (Lloyds TSB) there were thousands of 'hits' on the first day of their 2001 report.

Via a separate published report

A more common way of communicating the review of employment is through a traditional, paper-based, published report. This is clearly more expensive than via the Web but has the advantage of being a document that can be retained and saved by the individual.

As an addendum to the annual report

In the absence of the above two preferred methods, a 'people section' could also be included in the annual report and accounts. There is one anyway (executive remuneration and shareholding), so it isn't a completely new addition, merely an extension of existing practice.

The annual people report is a growing area of interest to organisations looking for comprehensive communication with their employees.

WHAT COULD GET IN THE WAY – BARRIERS TO COMMUNICATION

What the above has shown is not only the reasons behind the need for effective communication but also some of the ways it can be achieved. This wouldn't be an HR book, though, without the necessary balance, so I feel that I have to show some of the possible barriers to communication!

Poor communication happens when, *inter alia* (Guirdham 1999):

- the communication is intended but doesn't occur (ie the message is one-way)
- the hearer makes no sense of the message
- the information that is intended is not believed
- an attempt to persuade towards a particular direction fails
- an 'attempt to exert power fails.

It is important to recognise that there are likely to be barriers to communication in organisations and that these will have to be overcome in order for the communication to be successful.

Rouse and Rouse (2002) have identified such barriers as follows:

- socio-cultural barriers: groupthink, conflicting values and beliefs, stereotyping and ethno-centrism, language and jargon
- psychological barriers: filtering, perceptions, faulty memory, poor listening skills and emotional interference
- organisational barriers: information overload, message competition, information distortion, message-filtering, conflicting messages, status differences, structural problems.

When an organisation fails to overcome the barriers to communication the consequences can counter any strategic good work that has been put in place. Poor communication will lead to (Bland and Jackson 1991):

- a lack of understanding of company objectives
- the inability to carry out individual jobs to the highest possible standard
- a lack of perception of consumer demands and competitor challenges
- poor relationships with immediate superiors
- criticism and misunderstanding between different departments and divisions.

So there is a powerful case for getting employee communication right. The first part of this is to establish exactly what the organisation wants to communicate and, just as importantly, what the employee wants to know. Believe it or not, these two do not always tally.

CONCLUSION – TEN POINTS FOR EFFECTIVE EMPLOYEE COMMUNICATION

Employee communication remains one of the most challenging parts of the whole HR process. Its criticality lies in recognising its importance to the achievement of sustainable organisational success. The track record has not been good so far. There has been too little emphasis on engagement as opposed to downward communication. Evidence shows therefore that more effort needs to be put into developing the voice of the employee if true communication is to be achieved.

So, to sum up what have we learned from the evidence to date about how to communicate effectively with employees:

1 *Communication has to be two-way.* The first and most important principle to bear in mind – and probably the most ignored – is that effective communication is only truly effective if it is two-way. This means that upward and sideways feedback mechanisms need to be built in to organisational communication.

2 *Employees should be given a voice with which to speak as well as ears with which to listen.* This complements the first point and is something that is gaining increasing credence. Employee voice is not just a formal response mechanism to downward communication but a way of ensuring that the dialogue within the organisation takes place on an ongoing basis.

3 *Recognise that culture has an important part to play, and design communication accordingly.* This means that there is no one right way any more. It means that in a pluralist, media-driven society there is a wide variety of cultural considerations to be taken into account. These range from the type of language used to the way the communication is delivered. Recognising the cultural variations required to be effective will produce some enhancements. The minimum requirement here is to check each communication for the 'tone of voice' in which it is delivered.

4 *Use all available channels to communicate with employees.* There are two factors that make this an important point. First, the diversity of the workforce means that it is unlikely the organisation will have homogenous terms and conditions of service but instead a range of types of employee, from flexible to home to full-time. To reach them and give them a voice will require an equally diverse range of channels of communication. Second, the employee as citizen will expect to communicate using a range of channels. Yes, face to face will be the most common but written media, moving image (TV, video) and Web-based (e-mail, Internet, intranet) communication are expected. They should be used.

5 *Be original with people communication.* Earlier we saw that HR or people communication would have to compete with many other types of communication both internal to the organisation and outside it. The challenge facing the HR professional whose job is to engage employees in whatever aspect of people management is the subject of the communication is to ensure that his or her communication is the one that is received – both technically and actually. How can this be done? Well, one way is to do away with the typical dourness of the staff notice and replace it with a type of communication that is appropriately original. We're not talking about frivolity here, but something that can grab the attention of the intended recipient. The appropriateness comes because originality and bad news are not particularly good bed-fellows.

6 *Segment the intended 'audience' and design communication to fit the segment.* The organisation will reflect society – not a homogenous entity but one comprising a diverse set of people with diverse sets of expectations. For the communication to be effective it has to reflect this pretty fundamental point.

7 *Never underestimate the ability of the audience – or you will lose them.* Even when you have segmented the employee audience into like-minded and -voiced groups, don't underestimate their ability to grasp the point quickly. So don't patronise. (In case I might be doing that just now I'd better move on to the next point!)

8 *Don't assume that a single communication will be enough to transmit a message.* Multiple communications around the theme of the message, multiple channels and follow-up are essential. It takes time and effort to achieve successful employee engagement. It is rarely (if ever) achieved by a single piece of communication, however mind-blowing. Constant reinforcement is essential if the communication is to engage.

✱ 9 *Employees are very important customers of the organisation – treat them as such.* The HR communication should reflect this point. Shoddiness is no excuse. Haste and mistakes are unforgivable. It's incredible to me to see how little effort is put into employee marketing. By this I don't mean trying to sell them products but trying to engage them in the purpose of the organisation. It should be a top priority, and the communication should reflect this. Indeed, it should be at least as good a quality as that which goes out to the external customers of the organisation. Employees deserve it. And if they believe they are important they will deliver the business required, particularly the customer satisfaction on which so much competitiveness rests.

10 *Finally, always remember that the employee is a person with a life outside the organisation.* Believe it or not, there are other things going on in the world apart from this month's sales targets, however important they may be. So if a communication is to be distributed, try to avoid its conflicting with the personal life of the employee. You know the debate: should we communicate job cuts at Christmas? Why is the communication sent on a Friday? Why was it so difficult to decide what time to give off for Princess Diana's funeral? Get this sorted, or you will undermine any progress in the other areas.

There we are. Some guidelines. Please do with them what you will. Some will be relevant to your situation, others won't. But if we at least get the employee voice bit right, then the other stuff may begin to fall into place.

12

Developing effective HR communication to the board and senior managers

Simple phonetics. The science of speech. That's my profession. My Fair Lady (1964)

No strategy will ever be delivered without capable, committed and aligned people to bring it about. It is, therefore, imperative that high-quality input into maximising human performance is constantly available, is regularly given and is willingly taken by the top teams of organisations.

What part should human resource departments play in this context? The answer depends on the quality of their approach. I believe the core competence of HR functions within organisations has to be effective 'business partnering'. By this I mean a method of operating rather than specific roles. High-quality, cost-efficient service and administration provision, ie 'traditional' HR activity, will only serve as the 'ticket to the game' which could and maybe should eventually be outsourced to specialist providers who can provide the scale and investment to keep improvements coming. This would also leave 'business partnering' the space which is essential in order to shape, define and ensure delivery of human performance interventions that support business change and the achievement of strategic imperatives.

This is easily said; however, all activity within organisations is competing with other activity for money, resources and time. So how do human performance issues get established as a priority? How does HR business partnering get to be seen as real value-added?

Key themes

- Work to the corporate objectives, not your own.
- Fully understand the needs and the wants of the top team with which you work both collectively and as individuals.
- Build on delivery, not promises.
- Set up organisational feedback mechanisms that keep your messages on the table.
- Be opportunistic – scan for and quickly seize on the human dimension of problem-solving.

Even if you are not on the organisation chart as being in the top team, these things can help you establish yourself as part of the fabric of it. If you are in that top team they are equally important in order for you to influence the agenda. Mike Watts, HR Director, Scottish Widows

INTRODUCTION

It is essential that those in HR are in tune with the language and thinking of the main board so that we can understand the basis of its decisions and influence it. Naturally, the board of directors in the commercial sector or its equivalent governing counterpart in the public is a key audience for the HR community, and engaging it is an important facet of HR communication. We now know, as Jon Sparkes has outlined in his excellent summary of the role of HR at board level, that 'culture and other people issues have found their way to the centre of the corporate agenda' (Sparkes in Morton *et al* 2001). Those in HR have to be effective in persuading the board to support their strategy and policy on issues surrounding this agenda. In return HR has to meet the criteria by which board decisions are made.

Traditionally, the exposure of the HR function to the board was largely confined to remuneration (both the pay round and the pay of senior managers) and succession of the top team. Whereas these were important subjects, other HR matters were largely operational. Presentations to the board would consist of an annual review of achievements. In more recent times, however, competitive factors have forced a greater dialogue between the board and the HR function for the following reasons:

- The board of directors wants to see the big picture – how does the HR proposition fit in with the long-term direction of the organisation?

- Increasingly the board wants to be aware of any significant risks that may be associated with the achievement of the strategy. Leadership, employee motivation and retention fall into this category.

- The board is interested in all aspects of leadership and leadership succession. It will want to be confident that this is being directed well. HR have a clear role to play in this.

- The competition for scarce resources in the organisation is likely to be intense. A sound understanding of investment decision-making will be a prerequisite for those in HR seeking to gain board support and secure funds for its activities (this seems like a really Machiavellian point but it's just reality, I'm afraid).

- There is little likelihood of HR being given board approval as an act of faith. Instead, those in HR must be seen as aligned with business strategy and able to manage the company's resources in a business like fashion.

- The board of directors is concerned with supporting projects and initiatives that enhance the organisation's competitive position.

Each of these requires a level of communication between HR and the board that perhaps was not necessary a few years ago. Those who work in HR now need to understand the workings of the board, its role and purpose and how they may best meet these objectives.

THE ROLE OF THE BOARD

The role and constitution of boards are changing. Powerful forces are at work: 'the focus by institutional investors on the role of governance and the accelerating rate of turnover among CEOs are placing enormous pressure on boards ... These forces are likely to increase in strength over the next few years' (Lawler, Finegold, Benson and Conger 2002). Recent corporate collapse, US presidential announcements about the responsibility of boards, the recommendations of the ASB on corporate reporting and the board's responsibilities for approving these have continued a trend started by Cadbury. The significant change in the governance of organisations, the greater number of non-executive directors and, most importantly for those in HR, an increase in firms with a remuneration committee will have a real bearing on HR's involvement (Weir and Laing 2000). The focus on corporate governance is now acute. This means that boards of directors will themselves be reassessing whether their governance for meeting these new demands is as strong as it can be. One activity will be to make sure that all aspects of people governance are in order, both as a source of competitive advantage and as a mitigation of risk.

But what does a board of directors actually do? And how is this relevant to the HR professional in his or her new communication role?

HOW DO BOARDS OPERATE?

The board of directors of the organisation has four key responsibilities. First, it is accountable to the owners, shareholders and other stakeholders for *organisational performance* and to regulators for ensuring compliance with legislation. Second, it is responsible for *policy formulation* – creating a vision and setting values. Third, it is responsible for *strategic thinking* to set long-term corporate direction. Finally, it is responsible for *supervising management performance against business results*. An effective board of directors 'must be competent at integrating all four' (Garratt 2000).

In practice these translate into specific functions (Coulson-Thomas 1995):

- Determine a distinctive purpose for the company, a rationale for its continued existence, and articulate and share a compelling vision.

- Establish achievable and measurable objectives derived from the vision, and formulate a strategy for their achievement.

- Ensure that the company has adequate finance, people, organisation, supporting technology and management and business processes to implement the agreed strategy.

- Appoint a management team and establish the framework of policies and values within which management operates.

- Agree and review plans, and monitor performance against agreed targets, taking corrective action where appropriate.

- Safeguard the physical, financial and intellectual assets of the company and ensure ethical conduct.

- Report performance to various stakeholders in the company, particularly those with ownership rights and a legal entitlement to certain information.

We have seen what the essential purpose of the board of directors is. But how does it operate in practice, and what should the HR community do to ensure that the 'people voice' is given sufficient airtime in the competition for strategic resources? The Institute of Directors is the expert source on such matters; it has published some key aspects of how boards operate in practice (Taylor and Tricker 1991). Among these are:

- *collective responsibility*. The key point here is that the board manages as a committee, 'seeking to achieve a company view about an uncertain future and reach decisions by which all its members agree to be bound'. It will be imperative therefore for the HR professional with board responsibility to ensure that all the board members are convinced of the proposals in the HR strategy. Communicating these to the board as a committee that acts with collective responsibility is the key issue.

- *regular information for monitoring performance*. The board will want to see management accounts and statistical returns. Profit and cash flow are clearly two of the predominant pieces of information. However, there is an increasing demand for other qualitative information as well as quantitative. 'Are the employees motivated?' is a question to which the board will definitely want an answer.

- *information needed to review policy*. 'Boards should ensure that they have adequate information about underlying assumptions and particularly about the sensitivity of profits and cash flow to variations in those assumptions' (Taylor and Tricker 1991). Traditionally these assumptions have been about interest rates and market share. Now they are bound to include people assumptions. It is inconceivable that a modern board of directors would not want information about talent, leadership and succession that are as vital as any other assumptions. Again there is a strong HR obligation to deliver this information.

It is up to HR to produce its own strategies and policies that support the board's governing objectives. Equally, it's up to HR to communicate these policies to the board just as, say, marketing would communicate its customer service strategy.

WHO SITS ON THE BOARD?

The normal make-up of the board of directors is:

- the chair
- the chief executive or the managing director
- non-executive directors
- executive directors
- functional directors
- the company secretary.

In some organisations the HR director sits on the main board. Where this is the case the communication task should be more straightforward, because the director will be involved in the board debate on a regular basis and will have a feel for the 'mood' or the inclination of the board on any subject. Where there is no HR board member then it is usual for an executive director to take on the HR mantle in addition to other duties. In this case the communication challenge from HR to the board will be to ensure that enough priority is given to people issues by the executive director.

The challenge for HR in either situation will be to present people issues as being of strategic importance and to back them up with a business case that, where possible, satisfies the financial considerations or other hurdles that have been set. HR's position must be seen to contribute to competitive advantage and be understood to come from people with solid business acumen. It is unlikely that resources will be allocated to HR as an act of faith any more. Understanding the drivers of board decision-making will therefore be a critical component of the strategic competence of the HR professional. But is there a track record for HR in its board-level dialogue? No!

VOICES FROM THE BOARDROOM

So it's important that we gain board-level buy-in. How easy will that be? A starting point is to understand how well HR shows up on the board's radar. There is plenty of evidence to indicate how strong the signal is. A recent piece of research conducted by the CIPD analysed the views of directors about the HR function (Guest, King, Conway, Mitchie and Sheehan-Quinn 2001). The findings do not make pretty reading. The conclusions were as follows:

- Senior executives are not really aware of the research that shows the strong link between good people management and performance.
- Even when there was awareness, executives were sceptical of the research.
- HR directors are not often expected to play a proactive and strategic role.

Given this background then there is a good deal of work for HR to do if it is to ensure that its investment requests and business cases are accepted in a competitive resource environment. Communicating with the board is an essential part of this campaign.

We have a lot of work to do. When the personnel director of M&S left the board and was not directly replaced, it was noted that there was a view that 'the City did not care about personnel leaving the M&S board because the consensus was that personnel directors did not make money' (*People Management* 28 September 2000). My experience is that this view, if it did exist, will not be valid for much longer. Indeed there is growing evidence that the City and other external stakeholders in organisations will want to know more about the people strategies of an organisation – not less. *Ergo* there is a need for HR to increase its profile at board level, or at least at the level of the chief executive team (if not the main board), a point that is being acknowledged in organisations (*People Management* 26 October 2000).

INCREASING BOARD-LEVEL CREDIBILITY

The *Voices from the Boardroom* report was scathing about the calibre of HR professionals (Guest *et al* 2001). It noted that in the research findings there were exclusively negative comments about HR's strategic capability. HR was seen as an 'administrative bureaucracy'. Why is there such a negative response to a function whose speciality is the very resource that will lead to competitive advantage in the knowledge economy? Once again, as much as any other factor this has to be down to HR's self-perception and its unwillingness to take on board-level responsibility. An effective campaign to increase board-level credibility is therefore a priority, and communication will play a big part in it.

There is no magic formula for doing it. But there are some principles that may be applied:

- Get to understand the ways of the board in the organisation in which you work – what is its drivers, what is the decision-making process, who are the key players in the decisions?

- Present proposals in a way that is acceptable. If written reports are the norm, don't submit a photographic account of the benefits of a new employee relations strategy. Do a written report!

- Understand the timing of the HR presentation – don't try to get onto the agenda on the day that results are announced to the City and so on.

- Make sure that the board-level proposals are actually *strategic*. Don't confuse high-level operational requirements – eg a budget for a flexible benefits project – with strategic requests – eg a new strategy for diversity.

Information about people strategy and the effectiveness of good people strategy on the bottom line is now an essential part of HR's activity with the board.

Recently, *Global HR* magazine asked three advertising agencies to come up with campaigns to convince the board that HR made a vital contribution to the organisation (Beagrie, Boucher, Simpson and Peters 2002). The brief was perhaps a summary of what HR needs to do:

How HR wants to be seen: convincing the board of its merits

- to be a dynamic, credible force with business acumen that makes a positive contribution to the bottom line

- to be considered a priority – involved right at the beginning of any strategic agenda or business planning

- for business leaders to recognise the value of good people management and high-performance HR policies

- to be considered an effective business partner with a seat on the board

- to be seen as accessible and effective by the workforce, shedding the 'human remains' image.

Such a brief would seem to be the essence of what HR is trying to achieve in its board-level communication.

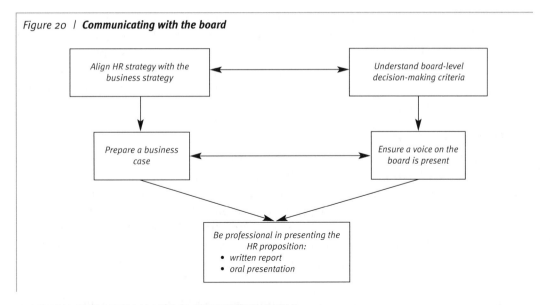

Figure 20 / **Communicating with the board**

A COMMUNICATION PLAN FOR THE BOARD

A possible sequence of preparing to communicate with the board is shown in Figure 20.

Align HR strategy with the business strategy – satisfying the triple agenda

This is a fundamental part of the role of those in HR. The changing nature of HR as outlined earlier in this book increasingly demands an HR strategy that satisfies the triple agenda of employees, the board and external stakeholders. Of particular relevance to the board will be to see that the HR strategy is aligned with the business strategy – especially when it comes to making budget allocation decisions. This is not to discount the interests of the board in other stakeholders. The board is always the ultimate guardian of the well-being of employees and the prime interface with external stakeholders (shareholders, the City, government), but for this part of the communications plan the alignment of the HR strategy with the business strategy is the prime focus.

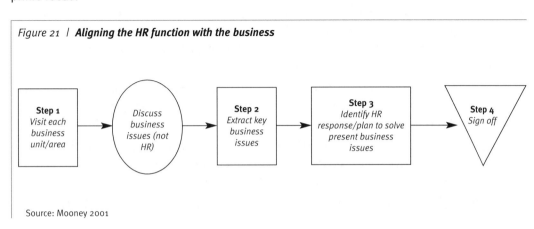

Figure 21 / **Aligning the HR function with the business**

Source: Mooney 2001

153

In his excellent book *Turbo-Charging the HR Function* Paul Mooney has outlined a plan for the alignment process, and this is shown in Figure 21 (Mooney 2001). This type of approach involves an initial dialogue with business areas and is followed by a value-adding response that has to be timely: it is no use HR giving well-thought-out and totally consulted plans that are not integrated with the overall strategy-setting process. It is essential that those in HR operate at the pace of the rest of the business.

Prepare a business case

It is no longer enough for the people aspect of the business strategy to be presented as an act of faith. It won't wash any more, and those in HR who aren't spending time 'commercialising' their approach won't get too far in this hard, measured world. The focus on human capital management has made this point even stronger than it ever was. It isn't such hard work any more, either. There is a wide array of facts and figures to demonstrate HR's contribution to the bottom line. One of the problems is that we in the function haven't been particularly good at shouting about them. The raised profile of human capital management and measurement will force this issue.

A brilliant model that can be used in the board presentation is the HR scorecard. This links people, strategy and organisational performance and is backed by the kind of statistical and financial measurement necessary when putting together business cases for consideration by the board or senior management team. The preparation of a business case is increasingly common for securing financial and other support for HR activity. The work by Becker *et al* (2001) analysed the top ten non-financial variables considered by financial analysts. These included management credibility, the ability to attract and retain talented people, and management expertise. As this type of research begins to filter through to the mainstream of management instead of remaining purely within the HR space, the board of directors will want business cases to support greater HR activity. Rather than signalling the demise of HR this will surely see the increased importance of the HR professional – if we get the business focus to be as good as our undoubted skill in understanding people issues.

Ensure that there is an HR voice on the board

The are a growing number of HR directors who have board-level status, as the importance of effective people strategies is recognised within organisations. In these cases it will be a straightforward matter for HR to be represented in the dialogue about strategy and resource allocation that will take place at board level.

However, it is not always the case that HR is directly represented. So there is an important communication challenge here: to make sure that there is an HR voice represented. There are several ways this can occur:

- Having a main board member with HR responsibility. If this is the case, then those in HR will have to have regular dialogue with the director concerned, raising issues and HR strategies that need to be discussed at board level.

- In the unlikely situation that a main board member does not have responsibility (the chairman or chief executive may take this on), then it will be up to those in HR to engineer a regular presentation to the board including: a standing item at the board meeting; issues-based HR presentations on pay, equal opportunities and so on; an HR plan and its progress; and a picture of the overall morale of the workforce. In some organisations an annual board presentation of the overall 'people' strategy is a useful way of pulling together the various strands of HR activity.

The debate about HR representation on the board has of course been rumbling along for a few years. Even now it's still raised as a deal-breaking issue – sometimes with an inexplicable *Schadenfreude*. Why people would want to keep banging on about this is beyond me, but there we are. What is absolutely clear is that HR has to have a voice at board level. Without it, the people aspects of the organisation may not get the chance for debate that they deserve. One way to achieve this is by those in HR understanding what goes on at the board and speaking the language of the board. In essence, this is effective communication.

Understand board-level decision-making criteria

What is the basis on which the board makes decisions? Understanding this and being able to communicate in a way that mirrors the process is a critical part of the HR communication process.

Coulson Thomas (1995) identified several characteristics of an effective board that illuminate how boards make decisions. Again, understanding this will be critical to HR's success in communicating effectively and ensuring sufficient focus and resources for the delivery of the HR strategy. He suggests the following questions about board effectiveness:

- *Do the members of the board share a common, clear, compelling vision?*
  It is likely that the board will use this vision as the basis of its decision-making. For HR activities to be given equal weight to other competing priorities there has to be a 'people' element to the vision. This means that HR will have to communicate the contribution that the people element will add to the overall success of the organisation.

- *Has the board identified what represents value for customers and the processes that deliver this value?*
  The board's decisions will obviously be influenced by the customer strategy. Resources will be allocated or approved by the board that contribute to the organisation's delivery of customer value. HR therefore will have to show that its own activities add value end to end, ie to the customers of the organisation. We know from Sear's research that a relationship exists between employee satisfaction and customer satisfaction, and many organisations are now building this into their decision-making criteria. Those in HR will have to communicate to the board, as a way of influencing its decisions, the impact of people strategies on its decisions to enhance customer value.

- *Are the directors committed to an agreed and realistic strategy for the achievement of the vision?*

The decisions of the board about strategy will be determined by the vision it has for the organisation. If this vision is to be, for example, 'the largest manufacturer of X in the world', then this will determine its strategy and how it allocates resources. Such a strategy may include international mergers and acquisitions, or major investment in global manufacturing sites. The HR professionals in the organisation will have to communicate their people strategies in support of this objective. Indeed, knowing the vision and the strategies should determine what HR actually does in its own strategic proposals.

- *Have the necessary resources, capabilities, skills, motivations, empowerment, roles, responsibilities and 'vital few' programmes for successful implementation been assembled?*

This is probably the most important aspect of the board's decision-making process for the HR professional. Communicating the fact that the HR strategies are part of the 'vital few' category of things that the board should be looking at on a regular basis is a significant challenge for those in HR. We have seen that the track record to date isn't particularly good. It should therefore be seen as a communication priority.

Be professional in presenting the HR proposition to the board

No one tells you how to present to the board. If you're in HR, the first board presentation is very much flying by the seat of your pants. However, effective board presentation can be crucial in determining whether the people strategy is accepted. Of course, there's no substitute for effective implementation but, believe me, don't underestimate the power of a good relationship with the board of directors.

Now we have a good understanding of what a board of directors does, how it makes its decisions and how it allocates resources to the various competing projects and strategies that are inevitable in the organisation. The next task we have is how to present the HR case in a way that it will command attention and ultimately lead to resource allocation. This is the essence of board-level communication. So what options do we have?

There are two main ways of interfacing with the board. The first will be through a written report and the second through some form of presentation. The main point to note here is the convention that the board adopts for either way of communicating. Understanding and matching this convention is highly recommended. Let's look at some of the options.

Written report

The overriding principle of a written report to the board is to follow the writing convention of board papers. This sounds obvious now, but the pressure of preparing the report may mean that the substance of the report dominates the process (as it should) but the form is overlooked. This will create an unnecessary focus on form, believe it or not. A ridiculous example: the HR report is in colour, on non-standard-sized paper with photographs. No other reports are submitted in this way. This could have one of two outcomes. The first is that the board may say, 'Hoorah for HR! How witty they've been to submit a report in this way. They're different, and we value difference in this organisation. In fact we need more.' The second is they may not say that. My vote would be for convention. This view is based on sound neuro-linguistic programming (NLP) techniques, in which we are trying to match language and steer the board to accept our proposition.

The written report should have these important qualities (Rouse and Rouse 2002):

- clarity
- precision
- vigour
- variety and rhythm
- emphasis.

Let's take an example of an HR report on senior manager pay. The format may be as follows:

- Executive summary – outlining the recommendation for pay, ie the conclusion first, the reasons for so doing, the costs and the benefits.
- The main body of the report should start with the background for dealing with senior manager pay; the reasons; comparisons with other organisations; market indicators and so on.
- Then a summary of the options that have been evaluated, showing the advantages and disadvantages of each.
- A recommendation should then be put forward as a defender.
- Detailed analyses should be included as appendices so as not to interfere with the flow of the argument.

This allows the board to see the big picture first and not have it slowly opened up to it like a fairy-tale for grown-ups.

Board presentation

The second area of board interface for those in HR is the presentation. This will hopefully be on a regular basis – perhaps tackling one issue at each board meeting, but there should always be an annual review of the organisation's people strategy as seen by the professionals.

The oral or visual presentation will have several key factors. I'm sure that anyone who has been on one of his or her own organisation's presentation courses and read any books or seen any videos about effective presentations will know that the key factors are the content, the style and the physical presentation.

For a board presentation the considerations will be as follows:

The content
The board is interested in what you are proposing. It may or may not be interested in how you reached the conclusion or the detail of your research. It is better therefore to present the proposition at a high level, with the conclusion or recommendation first. Keep the detail as back-up. Under no circumstances should you present an immensely detailed technical paper. The board isn't interested in how clever you are – although that may also come across! It is interested in how your proposal enhances the chances of achieving the organisation's vision.

The style

The style of the presentation will be organisation-specific. The only rule here is to make sure you don't contravene any of the fundamentals of style. This means you should: exclude the cheap and tacky; use stick men with discretion (ie don't); remember you are likely to be one agenda item out of ten or more – so brevity and succinctness are likely to be appreciated as a starter. If the board wants to engage in more dialogue, then that is fine. You should, though, bow to its needs and adapt your style accordingly.

The physical presentation

Again, it is better to accept the *mores* of the physical presentation requirements of the board (even if you don't agree with them). If you want to turn your presentation into a mime act, check this out beforehand. Most people will of course adopt the accepted style and stick with it – unless of course you have some personal crusade on dressing-down, culture change and so on. It may be fine to turn up to the board meeting in jeans and T-shirt but you really are better off presenting in the accepted style. Again, the idea is not to distract the board with your personal agenda but to persuade it that you, as an HR professional, know what you're doing in a business sense, know what the board wants and have a good story to tell. The less you distract it with your own quirks, the better (in my opinion).

So the written report and the presentation are two methods of interface with the board. Of course, there are many guides to report-writing and presentation style, and it is worth refining your own techniques through consulting these.

CONCLUSION

The communication with the board is as important for the HR professional as any other form of communication. Success in this area will produce the backing of the board – invaluable as you try to market the concepts into the rest of the organisation – and the resources needed to implement your proposals. So it is worth having a deliberate communication strategy for dealing with the board and making sure that this is a joined-up HR proposal. Which brings us nicely into the next chapter.

13

Joining-up HR through effective internal communication

What we've got here is a failure to communicate. Cool Hand Luke (1967)

There is no doubt that effective people management is critical to business success and that HR professionals play a major part in achieving that success. In any organisation, whatever the actual role of the HR professional, being an effective communicator is vital.

If we aren't clear about what we want to say to our colleagues, managers, trade unions and staff, how can we expect to work in partnership with them? Getting our message across effectively is important. We need to know that what we are saying is being understood in the way that we want it to be – that our clear frameworks and areas of flexibility are not seen by others as minefields of ambiguity or straitjackets offering no real discretion. Getting the language right for the audience is also critical, recognising that some words are emotive or even offensive will help, but properly checking understanding through feedback and confirmation is the key to success.

No effective communication takes place unless we also listen! As organisational experts we have a view about what works around here, but that is not the only view, and just as other people's understanding of what we are saying to them is important, so is ours of what they want to say to us.

So saying the right thing in the right way will help us communicate. But that isn't enough on its own. Are the messages that HR give clear? Do we have a joined-up approach to our people management issues, or does one policy contradict another; does our reward policy support behaviours that are integral to our vision, and is this backed up by our approach to training and development or are different approaches based on isolated ideals?

Effective communication is at the heart of effective HR and organisational success. Rita Sammons, County Personnel and Training Officer, Vice-President, CIPD

INTRODUCTION

It may sound straightforward, but it isn't. Getting the various parts of HR lined up and facing in the same direction so as to ensure that the communication strategy and plan are joined up will be as much of a challenge as any other part of the communication process. In fact, sometimes, getting the various parts of HR together is like herding cats! To illustrate the point, there was a (nameless) organisation in which, during a review of communication, all the HR materials that went into the public domain were placed on a conference table. These were things such as let-ters of appointment, job adverts, staff notices and so on. No two were the same. There were four sub-brands below the corporate logo. Some of the documents had no obvious branding or ref-erence – they could have come from anywhere. The language used looked as though it had come from different organisations rather than the same department. And the training materials reflected the preferences of each trainer rather than the branding and values of the organisation as a whole. The materials were basically a mess: unprofessional and inconsistent.

Now, I know that 'the slavish insistence on total consistency is out of date' (Morris 2000), but there have to be some guidelines about how the corporate values of employment are presented to a potential workforce – a workforce that has a good deal of choice about where it decides to work – or a board of directors that has investment choices about where to spend the organis-ation's money. The challenge to us will be to make sure that HR materials are as good as those issued by the organisation to market its products and services to external customers.

There are very good reasons we would want to make sure that the HR function had joined-up solutions that were communicated well:

- The effectiveness of HR communication could well determine the success or failure of the organisation, depending on how much engagement is achieved in the activities that the communication centres on.

- HR 'solutions' are complex and multifunctional. The pay award will involve reward, employee relations, communication activity, possibly training of line managers on market indicators and some HR policy input. Co-ordination and consistent communication of the outputs of these are vital to success.

- Employees and potential employees will expect professional communication on issues that affect their lives. HR has to respond to these expectations accordingly.

- HR communication is likely to be in 'competition' with a vast array of other internal and external communications. It will need to be outstanding if it is to stand out!

So, it is critical for the HR function to have joined-up thinking and practice, to have its people facing in the same direction, wherever they may work, to use consistent language with the right 'tone of voice' and to make sure that its communication plans are co-ordinated. In simplified terms we are looking to secure a virtuous circle of HR communications as outlined in Figure 22.

THE VIRTUOUS CIRCLE OF HR COMMUNICATION

So the objective we have in HR is to make sure that we communicate with each other. No big deal, you may think. But what does this mean in practice? The virtuous circle of HR communication shows some of the implications of this objective.

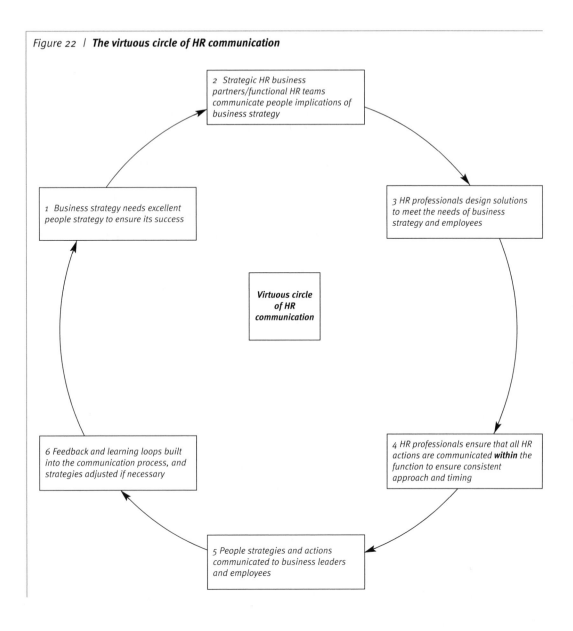

Figure 22 | *The virtuous circle of HR communication*

- The very first point is the most challenging of all. HR professionals have to persuade business leaders that unless as much time is given to the HR implications of business strategy as to (say) finance or marketing, then the chances of its succeeding will be diminished. And there is evidence to show that a truly joined-up and aligned business–people strategy can make a difference to the bottom line. An HR communication plan to make sure that this message gets through will go beyond the HR director working with the board, although this is clearly a critical activity. It will require all HR professionals within the organisation to be, dare I say, 'on message'. Without this first principle we don't stand a chance.

- Second, those in HR who work closest to the business (probably the strategic HR business partners) will have to communicate clearly and effectively their interpretation of what the business strategy is and what the people implications of this are. The two fundamental outputs of the strategic business partner will be the HR strategy for the division or business unit (to complement the organisation-wide HR strategy) and the HR plan. The first will determine policy implications, such as the reward basis of achieving the business strategy, and the second will determine resource allocation, such as recruiters, HR project managers and so on. The communication of both is a fundamental role of the strategic HR business partner. Without an effectively understood HR strategy the rest of HR will not be able to gear themselves up for delivery.

- The design of HR solutions is an area that will require the closest of communication between the various parts of HR. It will be no use the training design team coming up with training solutions for which there are not enough face-to face-trainers; no use the employee relations team coming up with new policies that the personnel professionals 'in the field' know nothing about; and no use the reward team designing a new pay package to be delivered in six weeks' time if the personnel professionals need eight weeks to cascade it. The interdepartmental communication process is vital to the success of the modern HR function because of the complexity and interdependency of the solutions needed.

- Effective communication within the HR function is also necessary to get a consistency of approach and to get the timing of the approach right. We want to make sure that the communication about training opportunities for all does not go out on the same day as redundancy notices; or that the notification to employee representatives about the establishment of a European Works Council does not go out the day after the staff notice announcing this. Co-ordination of the various actions required to deliver today's people strategies is a necessity.

- Of course, having designed these world-beating people policies and practices, we have to communicate them to the people to which they apply – the employees. We saw earlier that their expectations of how the organisation puts out its communication have changed significantly in this media-rich society. Therefore the HR communication should reflect the professionalism of the media to which everyone is exposed every day. The staff notice on the notice-board will no longer be enough to engage the employee, whatever the size of the organisation.

- Finally, given the fact that communication is a two-way process, the HR professional will have to take account of the need to give the employee a voice. This is as much a part of the HR communicator's job as designing the best people website or issuing effective cascade communication processes. It is not enough to provide outward communication. Incoming also has to be built into HR processes for them to be truly effective.

These general principles form the foundation on which communication within HR has to take place. However, what are the HR models that we are likely to work within? And what are the issues put forward by HR structures that can wither, get in the way of or enhance the process of communication within HR?

THE MODELS OF HR

It may be argued that if the 'governance' of HR was right then the communication would naturally fall into place. In this respect 'governance' means how HR is run and who has responsibility and accountability for HR activity. To answer this question I am proposing two models for HR:

- the strategic HR business partner/HR shared-services model
- the functional HR model.

This approach is not comprehensive: there are many variants. However, for the purposes of deciding on the best way to communicate within HR, these two should be enough to cover most of the principles. So what are the characteristics of the two models, and how may we best set up communication processes in each?

Strategic HR business partner/HR shared-services

In the post-Ulrich world the strategic HR business partner (SHRBP) who accesses HR from an HR shared-services provider (internal or external) is an approach to HR that has captured the imagination. In this approach the key business interface is provided by a SHRBP who translates the business strategy and manpower plan into people implications, and then decides on the HR services needed to satisfy these. HR strategy and policy may be included in this shared service but may also be a separate group within HR. An HR organisational structure that goes with this type of model is shown in Figure 23. The key responsibilities for each area are:

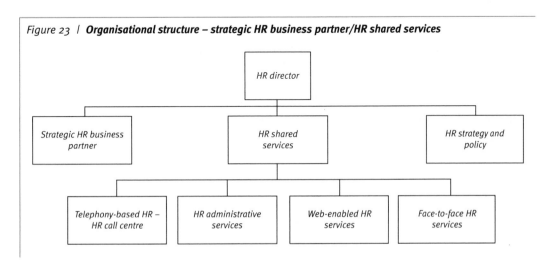

Figure 23 / *Organisational structure – strategic HR business partner/HR shared services*

- ### *Strategic HR business partner*

In this model the SHRBP is responsible for providing strategic HR support to the whole organis-ation, to a division or to a business unit. The SHRBP will be expected to contribute – as an equal partner – to the strategic business debate that takes place within the business unit and ensure that HR implications of strategy are anticipated. The two key tools of the SHRBP are the HR strat-egy for the unit and a manpower plan. These will enable the SHRBP to identify both HR policy implications and HR resource requirements. The SHRBP will then be required to secure either policy or expert personnel or training resources from a shared-services area.

- ### *HR shared services*

The HR shared services is a pool of all operational personnel and training people, expert HR 'technical' advisers (reward, equal opportunities), and administrative services (such as payroll) underpinned by new technology. It will be the responsibility of the HR professionals in the HR shared-services unit to meet the needs of the business as specified by the SHRBP and to pro-vide excellent personnel or training support. In addition there may be a policy role, if this is not a separate unit within the organisation.

This approach to running HR almost certainly came from the David Ulrich school of HRM and has been increasing in popularity for the past five years. Indeed, it is usual to have a SHRBP with or without the sharing of other HR services; by this I mean that whereas someone was once referred to as HR director, head of HR or senior manager HR, he or she may now have the title 'business partner'. The transition to the shared-services model for HR has been a feature of the past few years. Invariably, the success of the transition has been dependent on HR pro-fessionals communicating with each other. Standard Chartered Bank, for example, cited the communication process as a vital part of the establishment of their shared-services model around a new centre based in Chennai (Arkin 2002).

Functional HR

Even though the Ulrich revolution has certainly swept through HR functions throughout the world, there is still a large school of thought committed to functionally-based HR. Functional HR has some of the elements of the strategic HR business partner /HR shared-services model but is more rooted in the traditional (and still valid) way of running the function. Figure 24 shows a structure that may be encountered in this model: there is normally a business unit to which a personnel and training resource has been allocated – ie it is not shared – with a central policy and strategy team. In a multi-business-unit organisation there is usually some flexibility about whether to join in the overall HR strategy of a group.

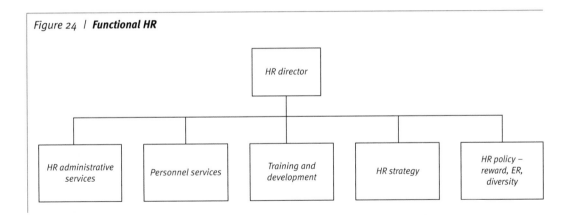

Figure 24 | **Functional HR**

The main characteristics of functional HR are:

- organisation along the lines of a technical speciality, ie personnel, training, reward, equal opportunities and so on
- dedicated resource to a particular business unit or area
- central strategy and policy-setting for HR.

This was of course the most common way to structure an HR function until Ulrich came along. It still is a very common method.

COMMUNICATION ISSUES WITHIN STRATEGIC HR BUSINESS PARTNER/HR SHARED SERVICES

The implementation of an SHRBP/HR shared-services model for HR brings with it a set of communication requirements that may be different from those encountered in previous models. Some of these are as follows:

- The SHRBP will have to be expert at identifying and communicating the organisational strategy. Because the SHRBP will be the main interface into the business, the ability to communicate what is going on, what the strategic direction is and what the implications of these are for the people in the organisation will determine the success or failure of HR. Then, the ability to translate these into clearly articulated project or 'business as usual' proposals will be paramount on the agenda. Without this clear communication the providers of the HR shared services will not have a clear plan of either volumes of activity or the technical nature of activity. Take recruitment as an example. If the SHRBP does not clarify how many people the organisation will recruit in the year ahead, then the HR shared-services provider will not be able to resource the recruitment team to the right levels. A breakdown of or poor communication in this area will eventually lead to poor recruitment or not enough recruits, and almost certainly failing to meet the deadlines required by the business unit concerned. The communication of strategy and specification of expected output is a key role of the SHRBP.

- The SHRBP will also have to be adept at spotting the policy implications of the business strategy. If he or she fails to do so and so fails to communicate these to the HR policy providers, then the organisation will move forward in its strategic direction with inappropriate people policies. An example here concerns pay. It may be that the organisation has a policy to pay engineers in the second quartile of an agreed pay benchmarking survey. But it decides it wants to upgrade its approach, and this means upping the pay scale to the third or even fourth quartile to get both the quantity and quality of engineers. If the SHRBP does not communicate this changed requirement to the reward policy professional, then the people response will be out of synch with the business strategy. Policy communication is as important as operational communication.

- The final communication issue in this type of structure is the need to join up all the diverse parts of HR. The SHRBP is the prime link into the business unit. He or she must be in constant communication with both the HR policy and the HR shared-services provider. A question that we must answer is 'What is the best vehicle for ensuring this communication?'

COMMUNICATION ISSUES WITHIN HR – FUNCTIONAL HR

The HR functional model will also have communication issues that need to be addressed if the objective of having a joined-up HR communication programme is to be realised:

- The first and foremost issue with this type of organisational structure concerns the contact between each of the functions – reward, employee relations, training and so on. Occasionally this type of HR model leads to a 'silo' mentality. After all, each of the HR functions will have its own objectives, and on any one day is likely to be faced with a barrage of demands from the business for its services. Often the frenzy with which business can operate on a daily basis means that intra-HR communication is not on the agenda: delivering the needs of the business is the prime responsibility. The issue here is the potential for fragmentation of HR solutions caused by the silo nature of HR functions.

- A second issue arises when there is more than one HR department in multi-business organisations. If Division or Department A has a particular set of HR needs, then it will be the prime role of the HR function of that unit to deliver them. But what if Division B has the same needs? It is possible that the HR function responsible for that division will deliver its divisional objective irrespective of the activity of the other HR team, leading to wastefulness and duplication.

- Third is the tension between the business unit and the overall people strategy, and how this can be resolved within HR. Who has the final say? The policy team operating with the board or the functional HR team working with the business unit? Yes, I know there shouldn't be such a tension, but it may arise.

In both the SHRBP and functional models of HR outlined above there are likely to be communication issues. Nowadays it's hard to imagine a situation where these issues will get in the way of the organisation's ability to achieve a sustained competitive position. Therefore they have to be resolved and HR has to deliver a joined-up response to business needs, of which an effective internal HR communication process will be one key element. Here are some ideas how this may be achieved.

A PROPOSED GOVERNANCE MODEL FOR HR

What can be done therefore to ensure that HR communication is joined up, does reflect business needs and is put over in a professional way? Let's start with the overall governance. What is needed is a forum and process by which the overall strategy for HR can be set, discussed, understood and bought into. Most organisations will have an HR senior team meeting, where the senior managers from within the function get together. This can be a useful vehicle if the meeting has the right focus. It is necessary, though, for this to be part of an holistic approach to the governance of HR. A proposal is included in Figure 25 that will be discussed in more detail below.

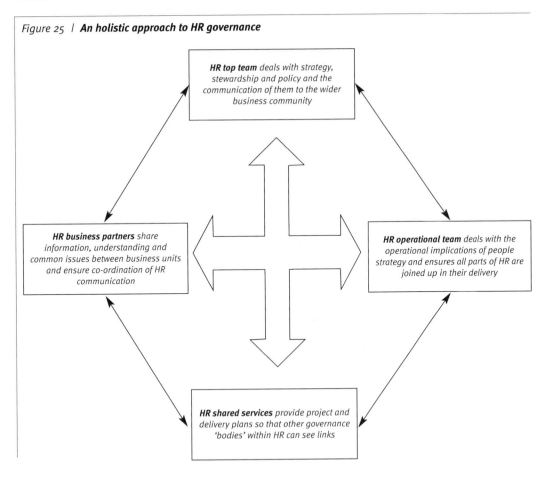

Figure 25 | *An holistic approach to HR governance*

HR top team deals with strategy, stewardship and policy and the communication of them to the wider business community

HR business partners share information, understanding and common issues between business units and ensure co-ordination of HR communication

HR operational team deals with the operational implications of people strategy and ensures all parts of HR are joined up in their delivery

HR shared services provide project and delivery plans so that other governance 'bodies' within HR can see links

The governance structure of HR is now something that will determine the success of HR. This is particularly true for effective communication. What is needed are clear 'up and down' governance processes and communication lines. As importantly, 'side to side' communication within HR will be critical – where HR business partners, policy and shared services interact. The following is a proposed governance structure to ensure this:

The HR top team

The HR top team should be responsible for setting a strategic direction for the function, agreeing objectives, and then monitoring their achievement. Using guidelines about running the board in the traditional definition, HR may undertake the following:

- Determine a compelling vision for the function.

- Establish measurable objectives derived from the vision and agree an HR strategy for their achievement.

- Make sure that the HR function has an adequate budget and people and organisational structures to support the demands placed upon HR.

- The HR top team are responsible for establishing a framework of HR policies and values which the management of HR would operate.

- The HR top team would agree and review plans and monitor performance against agreed targets (at a high level).

- The HR top team members would report on performance to the various stakeholders in the company.

We can see from the above that the HR top team would operate strategically and would take a high-level overview of performance against any agreed objectives. If the above role of the HR top team is agreed, then an agenda for each monthly meeting may look like this:

- review of performance against strategic objectives

- review of budget and headcount

- presentation of new HR policies (ie updates on European legislation, gender, race or disability)

- agreement of key communication messages

- agreement of HR communication strategy and plan

- agreement of roles and responsibilities within HR.

This team would provide the strategic framework within which the strategy and policy for HR would be determined aligned with that of the organisation and representing the position of the employee. Such governance would be an essential framework also for HR communication strategy and planning.

The HR operational team

At a level removed from the HR top team – although the two roles could be combined, as long as enough time was left for both strategy and operational HR issues (it's normally strategy that loses out at times of frantic activity – ie all of the time) – the role of the HR operational team could be as follows.

The HR operational team would be the operational arm of the HR top team. Its main roles might be:

- Define a customer service proposition and agree measures against which customer service can be monitored.
- Agree and review operational resource allocation to achieve HR objectives.
- Manage finance and headcount budgets that have been agreed by the HR top team.
- Ensure that there is sufficient training to meet the HR needs of the organisation.
- Agree an action plan for HR communication.
- Ensure interfaces between all parties to the communication.
- Agree and monitor application of HR brands, including the employment brand.

The HR operational team is a very different entity from the HR top team in that its focus will be on management as opposed to leadership and direction. It would not set strategy or policy but make sure that they were implemented.

STRATEGIC HR BUSINESS PARTNER/FUNCTIONAL TEAMS

These two forums will provide high-level strategic and operational governance for the HR function. In addition there will be other teams within HR with shared objectives. There is a need for consistency here as well. The first of these is between the business partner areas and/or functional teams. Here the communication responsibility will be about consistent message and implementation – a real challenge in multidivisional organisations. There are two ways this can be achieved. The formal will involve a regular briefing session between the SHRBPs or functional teams. This may be on a monthly basis with an agenda comprising:

- clarification of divisional or business-unit people strategy
- an update on progress in delivering the people implications of these strategies
- operational hot spots and the solutions for dealing with these (and any sharing of common operational problems for which a single solution may be appropriate)
- 'customer service' issues in which the customers are the employees or the senior managers of the organisation (and customer services measures will include staff attitudes).

Such an agenda will ensure a longitudinal view of issues and communication proposals that are both co-ordinated and consistent.

The informal communication between the SHRBPs is perhaps as important, and the most difficult to deal with because of time constraints and competing pressures. There is, however, a technological solution to this. The intranet or Internet can provide quick and easy access between the various areas; it is even better if some kind of bulletin board is set up so that common issues can be communicated and answers provided.

HR shared services/operational teams

Communication between the various parts of the shared-services providers will not be straightforward. This is because the modern shared-services model within HR is likely to consist of internal and outsourced providers. The challenge is to ensure that each of these providers knows what the others are up to, so that knowledge can be used productively. How can this be achieved? Of course, a regular dialogue is already likely to take place within each of the areas (so training will talk to training deliverers inside or outside the organisation; reward will talk to their providers and so on). What can be used to complement these communication channels is a forum of HR shared-services providers. Again, the monthly get-together is a good thing as long as it is focused, but the use of the Internet and bulletin boards as a way of knowledge-sharing is also a possibility.

CO-ORDINATED COMMUNICATION WITHIN HR

These, then, are some proposals for ensuring effective communication within the HR function. This section proposes a process for achieving this within these various forums or governance bodies.

Agree an HR strategy for the organisation

The first part of the process may seem a statement of the obvious but it does underpin just about everything else that goes on within HR. The agreement and communication of the HR strategy for the organisation are the platform on which the rest of HR activity should take place. Without it there is likely to be a series of tactical responses, which typified much of HR in the past. What is needed now is a strategic view of HR and this should be communicated throughout the function to give everyone a context within which their actions take place.

Agree an HR strategy for HR

Then we have to agree an HR strategy for HR. This means making sure that HR has a clear set of objectives aligned with the overall HR strategy, that resources are allocated to those parts of HR that need them to deliver the strategy, that measures of effectiveness for HR are understood, and that forums for knowledge-sharing and communication are put in place. There – it's easy, isn't it?

Ensure consultation within HR functional groups

Consultation and communication between the various parts of HR are critical to the success of the HR strategy. The above proposals, from the setting-up of an HR board to the various bulletin-board communications, are the means by which these are achieved.

Agree consistent messages and themes

Having established the strategy and structure and to some extent the processes by which HR can ensure effective communication, there is then a need to ensure consistency in approach. This means that if the training strategy is to move away from face-to-face towards Web-enabled or blended learning, then the reward strategy doesn't require huge amounts of classroom training for its success. This will be achieved by a consistent and common set of themes under-pinning both the strategy and the communication. Internal HR buy-in to these will come about through the same process by which employees buy into the business strategy: a two-way communication process matched by behaviour consistent with the stated strategy.

Agree regular checks on effectiveness

The final part of the process will be to ensure a regular dialogue about the progress of the HR strategy. This can be set against an agreed series of checks. Such checks may be against the objectives agreed for the overall function or those for individual members of HR. The balanced scorecard for HR is increasingly used as a mechanism for providing these checks.

CONCLUSION

There has never been a greater need to ensure effective internal communication. Indeed, some would argue that given the complexity of people strategy in the modern environment, HR's internal processes for communication have to be world-class. There is no doubt that this has become more difficult. The speed at which the HR function is expected to respond to business or organisational issues militates against communication and consultation. This can lead to fragmentation, inconsistency and poor delivery at the very time when we should be looking for the best use of resources, cohesiveness and six-sigma delivery.

The above proposals are not comprehensive and will not be applicable to every organisation. However, the principles on which they are based – ie there is a need to co-ordinate HR com-munication – is something that every organisation will have to deal with. Let us take the lead.

14

Conclusion

I've wrestled with reality for thirty-five years, and I'm happy, Doctor: I finally won over it.
Harvey (1950)

It's over 50 years since the *Harvard Business Review* published its classic article 'Barriers and gateways to communication' (Rogers and Roethlisberger 1952). Its authors wrote 'In thinking about the many barriers to personal communication, particularly those that are due to differences of background, experience and motivation, it seems to me extraordinary that any two persons can ever understand each other' (Rogers and Roethlisberger 1952). Remember, this was before the Web, diversity strategy and Generation X. As sure as eggs is eggs, the sentiment in the article has been compounded by recent social, political, economic and technological changes. In fact, we may conclude that the situation is far more complex than it was then. So it also follows that the solutions must be more sophisticated.

If we didn't have organisational noise, if we didn't have organisational politics, no bureaucracy, no rapid change, no Internet, then effective communication would *still* be a problem. The tone of voice or physical mannerisms (see Chapter 4) of a communicator may still distort a message. So imagine the challenges and hence the criticality of getting organisational communication right if you have to get employees behind a new strategy – or persuade the City and shareholders to buy your new executive succession plan, or convince the media that, no, there won't be any industrial action as a result of this year's pay award. Communication can be mindbogglingly difficult.

But there are things we can do, not only to mitigate the worst effects of distortion of communication but also to turn communication into something that adds real value.

The previous narrative has suggested that HR should have a greater stake in organisational communication than it has to date because:

- the expectations of HR's stakeholders have increased quite dramatically
- the Internet and new communication channels have created greater access to information and have therefore focused more attention on the communication of that information

- the nature of work has changed and the new 'contract' requires communication that is more open and advanced than that which went before

- corporate governance, as it has affected HR, demands more and better communication

- there is a cultural aspect to communication that requires HR's involvement.

However, this should not be a blanket process but one that is segmented into communication by:

- employees who work for the organisation and their trade union or representatives

- the senior management of the group

- the board

- the City

- the media

– and, of course, our colleagues in HR.

We also noted that there should be an HR communication strategy and an HR communication plan that allow those in HR to see the bigger picture and deploy their scarce resources effectively.

Finally, the concept of a two-way flow of information giving stakeholders a feedback mechanism (particularly giving employees a voice) is fundamental to success.

From this we may conclude some important guidelines for communication (Torrington and Hall 1991):

- The first concerns the sender, who should always have a clear idea of what exactly is being communicated.

- Then the purpose of the communication should be examined and understood.

- Given the influence of the environment on the communication, consideration should always be given to the total physical and human setting whenever you communicate.

- The planning of the communication should be thought through. If some of the influences on communication are understood then a better communication may result. Taking time to plan the communication in the first place will pay off. If necessary, consultation should take place with others who may have a different perception of the purpose, environment and method of communication.

- The fifth point is to be mindful, while you communicate, of the overtones as well as the basic content of your message. Remember that simple communication can be distorted by noise. It also takes place in an environmental context. There is plenty of scope here for different interpretation. Being aware of the overtones of the message will be a necessary part of the communication process. It can help to militate against misinterpretation.

- Finally, take the opportunity, when it arises, to convey something of help or value to the receiver.

But let's say we have all of these. There is still no cast-iron guarantee that communication will be effective. Something more is needed – two things, actually. First, an HR function that is competent in communication issues, that knows its stuff and that is able to persuade the rest of the organisation about the necessity of HR communication. Second, and perhaps as importantly, an HR function that is as passionate about communication as it is about training, diversity or well-being.

What we are trying to do here is, in the words of Kahlil Gibran, to turn the voice of the wind into a song. If you think this is a bit twee, fine. But look underneath the words to the sentiment. We are trying to convert all the strategic and operational noise that goes around in an organisation into words and actions that stakeholders can understand – that they can agree with, buy into, repeat to their colleagues, turn into action, build into objectives, bring to life, use in presentations, generate excitement through, find solace in, and explain reality and define relationships with. In the modern organisation communication requires an HR function competent in such matters and motivated to drive through a new approach. That is no mean challenge.

At the beginning of this chapter I referred to an article published in the *Harvard Business Review* in 1952 and noted that although events had moved on somewhat, the sentiment about the difficulty of communication still held good. Indeed, some of the solutions to good communication, in particular 'listening with understanding', have transcended time to remain good benchmarks for communication.

However, it won't be enough. Organisations have to do more if they are to engage their workforces, their senior managers and their boards. They also have to do more with the media and the shareholders. Those members of the organisation who are HR professionals have a valuable role to play in this push for effective communication. They are people experts and understand organisation dynamics. What's more, they are now an integral part of the senior management structure and are required to add strategic as well as operational value to the organisation's processes. Communication is both a strategic and business operational issue. HR's involvement has to embrace both these important issues. It is incumbent on the HR professional to do so.

We have to be careful not to 'weave air from air and remain without a garment', to quote Kahlil Gibran. We have to build a communication ethos that is solid. Good luck!

References

Accounting Standards Board (2002) *Operating and Financial Review*. Milton Keynes, Accountancy Books.

Accounting Standards Board (2002a) *Revision of the Statement 'Operating and Financial Review'*. London, Accounting Standards Board.

Adair J. (1989) *Great Leaders*. Guildford, Talbot Adair Press.

Adair J. (1997) *Effective Communication*. London, Pan Books.

Alberg R. (2002) 'Counting with numbers.' *People Management*. 10 January.

Allen R. K. (1977) *Organisation Management through Communication*. New York, Harper & Row.

Andrews P. H. *and* Baird J. E. (1989) communications for Business and the Professions. Iowa, Wm C Brown Publishers.

Aristotle (1991) *The Art of Rhetoric*. London, Penguin.

Arkin A. (2002) 'Satisfaction guaranteed.' *People Management*. 24 October.

Arkin A. (2002a) 'The package to India.' *People Management*. 24 January.

Arp C. *and* Gagneret P. Y. (2002) 'Is your people brand the brand your people are expecting?' HR Summit.

Armstrong M. *and* Baron A. (2002) *Strategic HRM*. London, CIPD.

Arnott M. (1987) 'Effective employee communication,' in Hart, below.

Baron N. S. (1999) *Alphabet to E-Mail*. London, Routledge.

Bartlett C. A. *and* Ghoshal S. (2002) 'Building competitive advantage through people.' *MIT Sloan Review*. Vol. 43, No. 2, winter.

Beagrie S., Boucher P., Simpson L. *and* Peters E. (2002) 'The hard sell.' *Global HR*. October.

Becker B. E., Huselid M. *and* Ulrich D. (2001) *The HR Scorecard*. Boston, Harvard Business School Press.

Bernstein D. (1984) *Company Image and Reality*. Eastbourne, Holt Rhinehart & Winston.

Betts M. (1999) *Strategic communication management – brand competence*. June–July.

Bevan R. *and* Bailey J. N. (1991) 'Employee relations,' in Lesley, below.

Birkinshaw J. *and* Crainer S. (2002) *Leadership the Sven-Göran Eriksson Way*. Oxford, Capstone Publishing.

Bland M. (1980) *Employee Communication in the 1980s*. London, Kogan Page.

Bland M. *and* Jackson P. (1990) *Effective Employee Communication*. London, Kogan Page.

Blundell R. (1988) *Effective Business Communication*. London, Prentice Hall.

Boisot M. (1994) *Information and Organisations*. London, HarperCollins.

Bowman P. (ed.) (1989) *Handbook of Financial Public Relations*. Oxford, Heinemann Professional Publishing.

Bragg M. (1996) *Reinventing Influence*. London, Pitman Publishing.

Brennan T. *and* Winter M. (2001) 'Communications technology – at what price?' *Internal Focus Magazine*. Smythe Dorward, Lambert. September–October.

Buckingham M. *and* Wilde R. (2001) 'Building a strengths-based organisation.' Harrogate, CIPD National Conference.

Byham W. C., Smith A. B. *and* Paese M. J. (2000) *Grow Your Own Leaders*. Pittsburgh, DDI Press.

Caldwell R. (2001) 'Champions, adapters, consultants and synergists: the new change agents in HRM.' *Human Resource Management Journal*. Vol. 11, No. 3.

Chapman C. (1991) *How the Stock Markets Work*. London, Century Business.

Chartered Institute of Personnel and Development – *see* CIPD

Chopra D. (2002) 'Maximising leadership potential.' Harrogate, CIPD National Conference.

Cipd (2000) *Effective People Management*. London, CIPD.

Cipd (2001) *The Change Agenda*. London, CIPD.

Cipd (2001a) *Voices from the Boardroom*. London, CIPD.

Clutterbuck D. (2002) *Does Communication Competence Contribute to Business Success?* Item.

Clutterbuck D. *and* Dearlove D. (1993) *Raising the Profile: Marketing the HR function*. London, IPM.

Conference Board, the (2002) *Value at Work: The risks and opportunities of human capital measurement and reporting.*

Conger J. (1998) 'The necessary art of persuasion.' *Harvard Business Review*. May–June.

Corporate Leadership Council (1999) *The Employment Brand*. Washington, Corporate Executive Board.

Corporate Leadership Council (1999a) *Transforming the Human Resources Function*. Washington, Corporate Executive Board.

Corporate Leadership Council (2002) *From Information to Insight*. Washington, Corporate Executive Board.

Corporate Leadership Council (2002a) *The Compelling Offer Revisited. Washington,* Corporate Executive Board.

Coulston Thomas C. J. (1995) 'Creating an effective board,' in *The Financial Times Handbook of Management,* London, Pitman Publishing.

Coupland D. (1996) *Microserfs*. New York, HarperCollins

Coyne K. *and* Witter J. W. (2002) 'Taking the mystery out of investor behaviour.' *Harvard Business Review*. September.

Daly E. (1999) 'Reporting from the front line,' in Glover, below.

d'Aprix R. (1982) *Communicating for Productivity.* New York, Harper & Row.

de Mare G. (1979) *Communication at the Top*. New York, John Wiley.

Deal T. E. *and* Kennedy A. A. (1982) *Corporate Cultures*. Reading, Massachusetts, Addison Wesley.

Domm D. R. (2001) 'Strategic vision: sustaining employee commitment.' *Business Strategy Review*. Vol. 12, Issue 4, winter.

DONKIN R. (2001), *Blood, Sweat and Tears*. London, Texere LLC.

DOWNES J. *and* GOODMAN J. E. (1991) *Dictionary of Finance and Investment Terms*. New York, Barron's Educational Series.

DURSCHMIED E. (1999) *The Hinge Factor*. London, Hodder & Stoughton.

FITZ ENZ J. (1997) *The 8 Practices of Exceptional Companies*. New York, American Management Association.

GALLIE D., FELSTEAD A. *and* GREEN F. (2002) 'Changing patterns of employee involvement.' *Skope Research Paper No 28*. ESRC-Funded Centre on Skills, Knowledge and Organisational Performance. Oxford and Warwick Universities.

GARRATT B. (2000) *The Learning Organisation*. London, HarperCollins.

GLOVER S. (ed.) (1999) *The Penguin Book of Journalism*. London, Penguin Books.

GOODRIDGE M. (2002) 'The crisis of organisation: ownership and meaning.' *Topics*. Issue 2.

GRAHAM J. (1995) 'Managing international public relations.' *The Financial Times Handbook of Management*. London, Pitman Publishing.

GRATTON L., HOPE-HAILEY V., STILES P. *and* TRUSS C. (1999) *Strategic Human Resource Management*. Oxford, Oxford University Press.

GRENSING-POPHAL L. (2002) 'Talk to me – when it comes to employee communication, it's sometimes better to receive than give.' SHRM online. 15 July.

GUEST D. *and* CONWAY N. (2002) 'Communicating the psychological contract: an employer perspective.' *Human Resource Management Journal*. Vol. 12, No. 2.

GUEST D., KING Z., CONWAY N., MITCHIE J. *and* SHEEHAN-QUINN M. (2001) *Voices from the Boardroom*. London, CIPD.

GUIRDHAM M. (1999) *Communicating across Cultures*. London, Macmillan Business.

GUMMER P. S. (1987) 'Financial public relations,' in Hart, below.

HAGGBLADE B. (1982) *Business Communication*. St Paul, Minnesota, West Publishing.

HANDY C. (1988) *Understanding Organisations*. London, Penguin Books.

HANSEN M. T. *and* DEIMLER M. S. (2001), 'Cutting costs while improving morale with B2E management.' *MIT Sloan Review*. Vol. 43, No. 1. Fall.

HART N. A. (ed.) (1987) *Effective Corporate Relations*. London, McGraw-Hill.

HARTLEY P. *and* BRUCKMANN C. (2002) *Business Communication*. London, Routledge.

HAYES ANDREWS P. *and* BIRD J. E. (1989) *Communication for Business and the Professions*. Dubuque, Iowa, Wm C Brown.

HEFTY R. W. (1991) 'Public relations and labour matters,' in Lesley, below.

HELLER R. (1988) *The Supermarketers*. London, Sidgwick & Jackson.

JEFKINS F. (1987) *Public Relations for Your Business*. London, Mercury Books.

KLEIN N. (2001) *No Logo*. London, HarperCollins.

KOTLER P. (1986) *Principles of Marketing*. New Jersey, Prentice Hall.

KOTLER P. *and* ARMSTRONG G. (1989) *Principles of Marketing*. New Jersey, Prentice Hall.

KRAMER M. G. (2001) *Business Communication in Context*. Upper Saddle River, New Jersey, Prentice Hall.

LAWLER III E. E., FINEGOLD D., BENSON G. *and* CONGER J. (2002) 'Adding value in the boardroom.' *MIT Sloan Management Review*. Vol. 43, No. 2, winter.

LECKIE R. (1990), *None Died in Vain*. New York, Harper Perrenial.

LENCIONI P. M. (2002) 'Make your values mean something.' *Harvard Business Review.* July.

LESLEY P. (1991) *The Handbook of Public Relations and Communications.* London, McGraw-Hill.

LIN N. (1973) *The Study of Human Communication.* Indianapolis, The Bobbs Merrill Company Inc.

LITTLE P. (1981) *Communication in Business.* London, Longman Group.

LEOPOLD J. (2002) *Human Resources in Organisations.* Harlow, Pearson Education.

MARCHINGTON M. (1995) 'Involvement and participation,' in John Storey (ed.), *Human Resource Management,* London, International Thomson Business Press.

MARCHINGTON M. (2001) 'Employee voice: new dimensions in employee involvement.' Harrogate, CIPD National Conference.

MARCHINGTON M. and WILKINSON A. (1998) *Core Personnel and Development.* London, IPD.

MACRAE C. (1991) *World Class Brands.* Wokingham, Addison Wesley Publishing.

McCOY C. (2002) 'Developing your people strategy.' Harrogate, CIPD National Conference.

MEAD S. (2002) 'Trade unions in partnership – a more trusting relationship?' *Topics.*

MILLER K. (1995) *Organisational Communication.* Belmont, California, Wadsworth Publishing Company.

MINTZBERG H. (1987) *Crafting Strategy.* Harvard Business Review. July–August.

MITCHELL P. (2001) 'E-mail versus face to face.' *Corporate Communication.*

MOONEY P. (2001) *Turbo-Charging the HR Function.* London, CIPD.

MORRIS S. (2000) *Wired Words.* London, Pearson Education.

MORTON C., NEWALL A. and SPARKES J. (2001) *Leading HR.* London, CIPD.

MOYNAGH M. and WORSLEY R. (2001) *Tomorrow's Workplace.* The Tomorrow Project, King's Lynn, Norfolk.

MUMBY-CROFT R. and WILLIAMS J. (2002) 'The concept of workplace marketing: a management development model for corporate and enterprise sectors.' *Strategic Change.* Vol. 11, No. 4, June–July.

MUNTER M. (1987) *Business Communication.* Englewood Cliffs, New Jersey, Prentice Hall.

MURPHY M. G. and MACKENZIE DAVEY K. (2002) 'Ambiguity, ambivalence and indifference in organisational values.' *Human Resource Management Journal.* Vol. 12, No. 1.

NEELY A., GRAY D., KENNERLEY M. and MARR B. (2001) *Measuring Corporate Management and Leadership.* A report commissioned by the Council for Excellence in Management and Leadership from the Centre for Business Performance at Cranfield Business School.

NORDSTROM K. and RIDDERSTRALE J. (2000) *Funky Business.* London, Pearson Education.

NORDSTROM K. and RIDDERSTRALE J. (2002) 'Business as usual.' Harrogate, CIPD National Conference.

O'DONNELL K. P., POWERS D. F. and McCARTHY J. (1972) *Johnny We Hardly Knew Ye.* Boston, Little, Brown.

OLIVER S. (1997) *Corporate Communication.* London, Kogan Page.

ORWELL G. (1972) 'Politics and the English language,' in *Inside the Whale and Other Essays,* Harmondsworth, Penguin.

PERKINS S. J. (1999) *Globalisation – The people dimension.* London, Kogan Page.

PFEFFER J. (1981) *Power in Organisations.* Stanford, HarperCollins.

PICKARD J. (2002) 'A global conversation.' *People Management.* 7 November.

Pigors P. *and* Myers C. A. (1969) *Personnel Administration.* New York, McGraw-Hill.

Pilger J. (1987) *Heroes.* London, Pan Books.

Porter M. E. (1980) *Competitive Strategy.* New York, The Free Press, Macmillan.

Porter M. E. (1985) *Competitive Advantage.* New York, The Free Press, Macmillan.

Porter M. E. (1990) *The Competitive Advantage of Nations.* London, Macmillan.

Porter M. E. (1996), 'What is strategy?' *Harvard Business Review.* November–December.

Porter M. E. (2001) 'Strategy and the Internet.' *Harvard Business Review.* March.

Purcell J. (2001) 'Personnel and human resource managers: power, prestige and potential.' *Human Resource Management Journal.* Vol. 11, No. 3.

Quirke B. (2002) 'An interview with Bill Quirke.' *Corporate Communication.* Melcrum Online.

Quirke B. (2002A) 'Communication breakdown.' *Global HR.* June.

Rainbow P. (ed.) (1984) *The Foucault Reader.* London, Penguin.

Rana E. (2002) 'Flying information.' *People Management.* 7 November.

Remnick D. (1999), *King of the World.* London, Picador.

Rogers C. F. *and* Roethlisberger F. J. (1952) 'Barriers and gateways to communication.' *Harvard Business Review.* July–August.

Rouse M. J. *and* Rouse S. (2002) *Business Communications.* London, Thomson Learning.

Rucci A. J., Kirn S. P. *and* Quinn R. T. (1998) 'The employee-customer-profit chain at Sears.' *Harvard Business Review.* January–February.

Sampson A. (1995) *Company Man.* London, HarperCollins.

Scholes E. (1999) *Guide to Internal Communication.* Aldershot, Gower Publishing.

Segars A. H. *and* Kohut G. F. (2001) 'Strategic communication through the World Wide Web: an empirical model of effectiveness in the CEO's letter to shareholders.' *Journal of Management Studies.* Vol. 38, No. 4, June. pp535–556.

Skellon N. (1999) *Corporate Combat.* London, Nicholas Brealey.

Sloman M. (2001) *The E-Learning Revolution.* London, CIPD.

Smith P. (1989) 'Professionals and institutions,' in Bowman, above.

Smythe J. (2002) 'The rise and rise of the internal communicator.' Profile *IPR Magazine.* May.

Stevenson N. (2002) *Understanding Media Cultures.* London, Sage.

Taylor B. *and* Tricker B. (1991) *The Directors' Manual.* Cambridge, Director Books.

Thomson K. (1990) *The Employee Revolution.* London, Pitman Publishing.

Timm P. R. (1986) *Managerial Communication.* Englewood Cliffs, New Jersey, Prentice Hall.

Torrington D. *and* Hall L. (1991) *Personnel Management.* New York, Prentice Hall.

Truss C. *Strategic Human Resource Management.* Oxford, Oxford University Press.

Turner P. (2000) *Achieving and Maintaining the Human Advantage in Organisations: The role of HR 1979–1997 and beyond.* Nottingham, NBS Papers, Professional Paper Number 1.

Turner P. (2002) *HR Forecasting and Planning.* London, CIPD.

Udall R. *and* Udall S. (1982) *People and Communication.* Hulton Educational Publications.

Ulrich D. (1996) Human Resource Champions. Boston, Harvard Business School Press.

Ulrich D. (1998) 'A new mandate for human resources.' *Harvard Business Review.* January–February.

van Riel C. B. M. (1992) *Principles of Corporate Communication.* London, Prentice Hall.

Vardman G. T. *and* Vardman P. B. (1973) *Communication in Modern Organisations.* New York, John Wiley.

WAITLEY D. (1995) *Empires of the Mind.* London, New York, BCA.

WALTERS H., MACKIE P. and R., *and* BACON A. (1997) *Global Challenge.* Sussex, The Book Guild.

WEFORD A. (1987) 'Planning for corporate communication,' in Hart, above.

WEIR C. *and* LAING D. (2000) 'The performance–governance relationship: the effects of Cadbury compliance on UK-quoted companies.' *Journal of Management and Governance.* Vol. 4, No. 4.

WHITTINGTON R. *and* MAYER M. (2002) *Organising for Success in the Twenty-First Century.* London, CIPD.

WHITTINGTON R., MAYER M. *and* SMITH A. (2002) 'The shape of things to come.' *People Management.* 10 October.

WILLIAMS C. (1989) 'Media relations,' in Bowman, above.

WILSON A. N. (1999) 'Reviewers I have known,' in Glover, above.

Suggested reading resources

1 *People Management*, Published by the Charatered Institute of Peronnel and Development, London
2 *Fast Company*, Published by Fast Company, Boston, MA, USA
3 *HR News*, Published by the Society for Human Resource Management
4 *HR Magazine*, Published by the Society for Human Resource Management
5 *Financial Times*
6 *MIT Sloan Review*
7 *Harvard Business Review*
8 *Human Resource Management Journal*
9 *Strategic Change*
10 *Sunday Times*
11 *Evening Standard*
12 *Workplace Visions*
13 *Daily Mail*
14 *Daily Mirror*
15 *New York Times*
16 *Global HR*

Index